LEFT BANK

#3

Sex
•
Family
•
Tribe

BLUE HERON PUBLISHING, INC.
HILLSBORO, OREGON

Editor: Linny Stovall
Associate Editor: Stephen J. Beard
Publisher: Dennis Stovall
Staff: Holly Santos, Mary Jo Schimelpfenig, William Woodall
Advertising: John Johnson
Interior Design: Dennis Stovall
Cover Design: Marcia Barrentine
Advisors: Ann Chandonnet, Madeline DeFrees, Katherine Dunn, Jim
          Hepworth, Ursula Le Guin, Lynda Sexson, J.T. Stewart, Alan
          Twigg, Lyle Weis, Shawn Wong

Editorial correspondence: Linny Stovall or Stephen Beard, Left Bank,
Blue Heron Publishing, Inc., 24450 N.W. Hansen Road, Hillsboro, OR
97124. Submissions are welcome if accompanied by a stamped, self-
addressed envelope. Otherwise they will not be returned. Authors must
have a strong connection to the Pacific Northwest. Submissions are read
two months before deadline. Editorial guidelines are available on re-
quest (include SASE).

Left Bank, a series of anthologies, is published semiannually by Blue
Heron Publishing, Inc., 24450 N.W. Hansen Road, Hillsboro, OR
97124. Subscriptions are $14 per year (postage included). Single issues
are $7.95 (plus $2 s&h). Left Bank is distributed to the book trade
and libraries in the United States by Consortium Book Sales and Dis-
tribution, 287 East Sixth Street, Suite 365, Saint Paul, MN 55101.

Rights & permissions: © 1991 by Margaret Dragu. Reprinted from
Mothers Talk Back by permission of Coach House Press. In the United
States order from InBook, PO Box 120261, East Haven, CT, 06512. In
Canada order from Stewart House, 380 Esna Park Drive, Markham,
ON, L3R 1H5.

Alexis Seniantha, Dene Tha', Assumption Reserve from *THOSE WHO
KNOW: Profiles of Alberta's Native Elders* (1991) by Dianne Meili is
reprinted by permission of NeWest Publishers Ltd. Edmonton, Alberta,
Canada.

Cover and accompanying inside art by Lori-ann Latrèmouille (pages 60,
61, 129, and 141).

LEFT BANK #3: Sex, Family, Tribe, Winter 1992
Copyright © 1992 by Blue Heron Publishing, Inc.

ISBN 0-936085-53-3
ISSN 1056-7429

Contents

Introduction 5

WHAT WE CALL EACH OTHER
Anndee Hochman 7

INTRODUCING MYSELF
Ursula K. Le Guin 12

FEMINISM REVISED
René Denfeld 16

THE BUTCHER'S EAR
Colleen J. McElroy 22

PHOTO ESSAY
Marsha Burns 31

THE INITIATION: A MEMOIR OF SPAIN, 1964
Judith Barrington 39

FOOD FOR THE DEAD
Kathleen Tyau 46

BARBIE TELLS HER BIOGRAPHY
Lucia Maria Perillo 47

CLOCK PUNCHERS
David James Duncan 48

MOMZ RADIO
Margaret Dragu 56

MY NEW FATHER
Martha Gies 62

LEAVING HOME
William Stafford 68

SOMETHING THAT HAPPENS RIGHT NOW
William Stafford 69

LA MORENA
Kathleen J. Alcalá 70

GETTING IN AND OUT OF HATE GROUPS
James A. Aho 78

Why We Are Afraid
    Clemens Starck 85

"I Believe in Reason..." An Interview with Charles Johnson
    Andy Helman 86

Woman of the Bus
    Omar S. Castañeda 92

Life in Hell: It Isn't You
    Matt Groening 97

Tribes and Diatribes
    Doug Marx 98

Bark Us All Bow-Wows of Folly
    Ken Kesey 104

Tribal Life
    Lawson Fusao Inada 112

Life in Hell: ...Family Values
    Matt Groening 116

Alexis Seniantha : Dene Tha', Assumption Reserve
    Diane Meili 117

Walkabout
    Bill Witherup 125

Sleeping Alone
    William Kittredge 130

Mercy
    Evelyn Lau 135

The Moves to Shrink the Distances (for Rosa)
    Duane Niatum 140

So What if the Neighbors Aren't Home
    Peter Sears 142

Down a Well
    Peter Sears 143

Credits
   145

I remember every detail that day when my 17 year-old babysitter warned me about being a girl. She'd rather be a boy, she said, being a girl was the pits. I see the apple tree crotch she straddled, the jeans and sweatshirt she wore, and me sitting cross-legged on the orchard grass beneath her. I was 11 and the moment burned deeply into my psyche. I had no idea such things could be talked about, nor what lay ahead.

So much about the way we lived in the '50s was unconscious. In those days, we had genuine nuclear families, though we didn't know to call them that. Like many North Americans after the upheaval of the Great Depression, my parents were hard at work establishing a solid economic life — building a home in the suburbs, entering professional life, and for the most part, maintaining inherited ways. My family included a mother and father together for the duration, three daughters, grandmothers and cousins who visited, and lots of dogs, chickens, and pigs. It all looked pretty regular. The connective tissue of cultural and ethnic tradition was still taut.

Later I would see that my sisters and I formed a spectrum. I was a tom-boy — even before my babysitter hinted at the wonders of cross-overs — one of my sisters was a lesbian, and the other sweet on pink dresses. While we were atheists, the Jewish heritage on one side of the family ensured that as kids we had a semblance of clan life.

Today, our allegiances, our connections to one another, and our relationships within our immediate and extended families are all up for examination and rearrangement. In the course of change, whether that entails breaking with family and religious traditions, or severing the silence of abuse, or rioting in the streets, some have found further barriers and turmoil. For others, loosening the connective tissue has unveiled opportunities for new arrangements and celebrations.

In this issue, we share with you the barriers and turmoil, the new arrangements and celebrations now existing alongside and in many cases complementing the old cultural and ethnic traditions. Peter Sears and Duane Niatum celebrate the great constants of love and passion. William Kittredge wraps a contemporary Western around a reminder of the awkwardness of innocence. Evelyn Lau and Omar Castañeda, by contrast, draw us to the nether worlds of sex, bringing strangely tender sensibilities to tough subjects.

Ursula K. Le Guin, Judith Barrantine, and Margaret Dragu explore issues and perspectives on culture and gender, and René Denfield slaps the tenets of post-Reagan feminism, while Martha Geis adapts a new cultural mode, finding a father in the guise of a newborn.

On the tribal front, Doug Marx lambastes white guys looking in all the wrong places for their identity. Sociologist James Aho guides us to the edges of our culture in his examination of the motivations and influences on right wing Christian Patriots, revealing the fluidity of movement in and out of those groups. Diane Meili introduces us to a gentle native elder, a man who maintains the ancient perspectives and soothing rituals of life on Canada's northern plains.

There is more — excerpts from new novels by David James Duncan and Ken Kesey, poems from William Stafford, biting cartoons from Matt Groening, a recollection of an international kinship from Colleen J. McElroy, an enlightening interview with Charles Johnson. And yet more from poet Clemens Starck, photographer Marsha Burns, artist Lori-ann Latrèmouille, short-fictionist Kathleen J. Alcalá, and essayists Lawson Fusao Inada and Bill Witherup.

Anndee Hochman's wonderful exploration of language in "What We Call Each Other" leads this edition by way of summarizing the changes in the way we name our relationships. She ends with: "Welcome, I might say, to my tribe. My group. Cabal. Circle. Club. Nucleus. Team. Neighborhood...Household. Brood. Collection. Cronies."

And welcome we might say, to sex, family, tribe.

Linny Stovall

W e'd covered all the routine subjects — the weather in Portland, the weather in Ventnor (it was summer in both places). I'd thanked him for sending me a paperback copy of *The Joys of Yiddish*. Then my 89-year-old grandfather said, "So, how's your lady friend?"

I gulped. It was possible he meant my roommate, Rachael, and "lady friend" was a quaint attempt to cover up the fact that he'd for-gotten her name. But I'd never heard him use that phrase, with its tinge of old-fashioned, coy romance, to describe an acquaintance of mine.

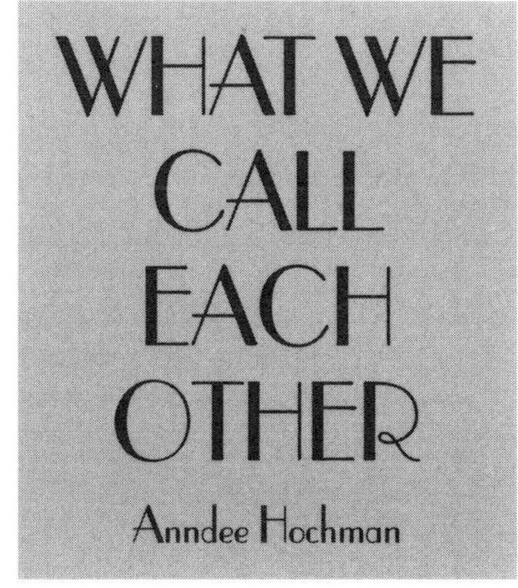

Finally, I mumbled that she was just fine, thanks. "Rachael and John are fine, too," I said, testing. There was no response.

Later, I told my "lady friend" about the comment, and we both laughed. But I still don't know if my grandfather knew what he asked, if he grasped what he heard. Words are like that. They can swab the air clean of illusion or they can fog the truth in a comfy, opaque veil.

So many of the words for romantic or sexual partners make women mere appendages of men, extend a longstanding power imbalance. What is the term to describe a relationship of equals, two adults trying to make a life together? I like "partner," with its hints of adventure and readiness, the idea of moving together through a love affair or a life. Most of my friends, gay or straight, use it to describe their romantic associates.

But even "partner" isn't perfect. For one thing, it conveys a sense of stability that doesn't apply to all relationships, especially brand-new ones. Heterosexual couples have a whole vocabulary that hints at changing degrees of intimacy and intention. First "lovers" or "boy-friend/girlfriend"; then "fiancé/e"; finally "spouse." But unmarried or gay partners have no language to describe those shifts.

The words commonly used in such cases are designed to mask the truth rather than tell it. The euphemisms for gay and lesbian lovers — "constant companion" or "very special friend" — hide the true nature of the relationship under a cloak of decorum. But it's a cloak made to be seen through; everyone knows it's a cover for something else. It indicates that the real thing is too scandalous even for dis-

course; the word itself can't go out of doors unclad.

One lesbian couple I know dislikes "partner" for the same reasons I'm drawn to it — because it is democratic, gender-neutral. These women refer to each other as "girlfriends," refusing, even in casual conversation, to pass.

Slowly, slowly, names gather a new history; the weight of a word can shift. When lesbians and gay men appropriate the language of the mainstream, filling in their partners' names where government forms say "spouse," insisting to the zoo cashier that they deserve a "family" membership, they force others to reorder their mental maps. Those maps would change even faster if heterosexual couples boycotted marriage and its honorifics, if they, too, combed the language for words that more precisely describe their bonds.

Girlfriend. Boyfriend. Mistress. Beau. Wife. Old man. Lady friend. Steady. Better half. Little woman. Helpmate. Hubby. Fiance. Lover. Paramour. Spouse. Domestic partner. Soul-mate. Significant other. Co-habitant. Ally. Longtime companion. Accomplice. Live-in. Partner. Associate. Collaborator. Consort. Intimate. Confidant/e. Familiar. Alter ego. Mainstay. Second self. Complement. Mate.

Even words that don't carry a gender bias can be suspect, quiet enforcers of the status quo. I used the word "single" to describe women without intimate partners until the irony of the term struck me. I was writing about these women precisely because they'd built networks of support through work, friends, housemates, yet my easy description of them conveyed someone alone and unconnected, with no important social ties.

"Are you in a relationship?" people inquire euphemistically, when what they mean is "Are you sexually involved with someone?" The notion of *a* relationship — primary, intimate, more weighty than the rest — doesn't fit the lives of people who choose celibacy, or who are in non-monogamous relationships involving two or more significant "others."

I thought of Guadalupe Guajardo's response to inquiries about whether she was "in a relationship" from people who do not know she is a nun.

"I'm in lots of relationships," she answers, and watches their eyebrows lift in surprise.

Then there's "friend," which doesn't begin to cover enough ground. It describes everyone from the colleague I chat with once a month at

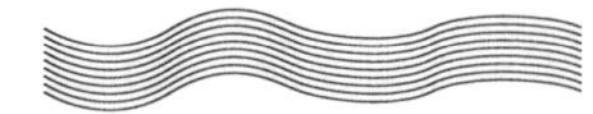

a writers' meeting to the woman I've known since infancy, but haven't seen since 1983, to Rachael, whom I've lived with for almost five years. The word, forced to stand for such a range of connections, erases distinction, implies all friendships are the same.

Names wake us to the particulars of a thing. If I call Diana my mainstay, Pattie my soul-mate and Rachael my sister, I remember that these women have different qualities, that my friendship with each is unique.

I say Rachael is my "sister," and then pause. Why is that the only term that seems to fit? I struggle to describe closeness and am left holding a simile, a stand-in phrase that only gropes at description. "He's like a brother to me," we say, revealing not only the assumed potency of sibling bonds but the dearth of words to describe intense, non-sexual attachments.

There's a level of intimacy that "friend" seems too small to contain. Then we make it even smaller, often denigrating it with the qualifier "just." They're "just friends," we concede, as if friendship were automatic and uninteresting, less full of potential than any romantic pairing. In fact, the vast majority of people in our lives fall into that maligned category; friendship deserves a vocabulary of its own.

Acquaintance. Colleague. Buddy. Bosom-buddy. Sidekick. Chum. Amiga. Compadre. Homeboy. Mate. Pal. Sister. Fellow. Brother-in-arms. Right-hand-man. Companion. Companera. Associate. Cohort. Crony. Aficionado. Compeer. Confrere. Ally. Comrade. Familiar. Accomplice. Mainstay. Primary. Neighbor. Friend.

I've wrestled, too, with "childless." It's a gender-weighted word; we don't refer, with quite the same sense of anomaly and pity, to "childless" men. It assumes childbearing is the norm and *not* childbearing is a lesser version of life; it defines an existence by what it lacks. "Non-parent" makes the same mistake.

I've seen women use "child-free," which seems tipped in the other direction — as though children were a burden and only people without them have liberty. Besides, many women who choose not to be parents include children in their lives as nieces and nephews, neighbors, clients, friends. I thought about words like "adult-based," or "adult-centered," for women who don't have much to do with children. But I've yet to find a term that expresses, without judgment, the facets of this complicated choice.

And there are relationships, existences we scarcely have language

to describe. The words for unmarried women — spinster, old maid — are all pejorative. "Old maid," in particular, holds layers of judgment — a woman who contradicts her own nature, at once old and young, a perpetual servant. Thanks to Mary Daly and others, women are reclaiming "spinster" as a source of creative pride; one friend I know named her sewing business "Spinster Textiles."

Few terms exist to describe former lovers who now are good friends, or non-biological parents, or relationships between the childhood families of a gay couple. I've heard a woman explain to her child, conceived through alternative (as opposed to "artificial") insemination, that there are "seed daddies" as well as the kind of daddies who live at home, and a lesbian friend coined "sister-outlaws" to describe her lover's siblings.

The contemporary women's movement and gay/lesbian liberation helped prompt people to create new honorifics, such as "Ms," and reclaim old names, taking them back from the domain of those who hate. Spinster. Dyke. Crone. Cripple. Faggot. Fat person. Fairy. When we use these words for ourselves, we become powerful, filled with the awesome responsibility that is naming. We print the words on buttons, shout them in parades. We repossess the names and, in the process, repossess ourselves.

Language changes from the edges; new terms ripple back to the center. Gradually, I have seen "partner" replace "longtime companion" in news stories about gay men and lesbians. Several papers even have begun listing gay commitment ceremonies. As such events become more popular and public, terms unimagined as yet may enter the lexicon.

Marriage. Engagement. Nuptials. Wedlock. Conjugal tie. Hitching. Coupling. Espousals. Union. Match. Bond. Pairing. Knot. Joining. Dovetailing. Commitment ceremony. Intentional. Dedication. Webbing ritual. Mingling. Intertwining. Weaving. Blending. Concord. Alignment. Alchemy. Convergence. Hand-fasting. Tryst.

What we call each other — how we refer to lovers and friends, partnerships and families — is more than a matter of etiquette. The words tell us who is owned and who is free, who really counts and who is merely secondary.

The language of the nuclear family continues to sway our speech, crowd out equally valid models of living. I work with homeless teenagers, who take the words of the families that failed them and apply

them to each other. I've heard them use "sister" and "brother" for their friends, but also "mother" and "kid," outlining large and intricate networks of street kin.

The actual people represented by those terms may have abused or abandoned these teenagers, but the words themselves seem to carry an infinitely renewable potency, a hope that someday someone will grow into the legend that is "mother," "sister" or "son."

"Blood family" itself carries that mythic power — "blood," with its symbolism of oath and source, a magical connection that cannot be undone. "Biological family" is less poetic but equally weighted. Married couples aren't related genetically, nor are adopted children. In families formed through remarriage, in foster families and extended families, "blood" connections have little to do with linkage.

I've toyed with "first family," "original family" and "childhood family" to describe the groups we grow up with, and "present family," "chosen family" or "adult family" for those we have now.

But the word "family" itself is loaded. The term can help justify secrecy ("Let's keep it in the family") or serve as an argument for public hands-off ("That's a family matter.") And it is used disingenuously, as in "We're all one big happy family here," by businesses that want to promote childlike docility from employees and avuncular rule from bosses.

No mere noun, it's a way of categorizing society, even allocating resources, with "family" memberships and "family" fares on airlines and trains. "Family values" is political shorthand, evoking marriage, patriotism and obedient children, a code aimed to rally a changing world.

Imagination is larger than language. The names claim who we already are and who we wish to become. We don't require them in order to live, but they make our living known, translatable, turn it into something we can talk about. There is room for more words, for the finest of distinctions, for as many possibilities as our minds can shape.

Welcome, I might say, to my tribe. My group. Cabal. Circle. Club. Nucleus. Team. Neighborhood. Community. Affinity group. Kin. Karass. Familiars. People. Coalition. League. Assemblage. Confederation. Gang. Clique. Coterie. Set. Crew. Crowd. Cadre. We-group. Affiliates. Relations. Folk. Kindred. Household. Brood. Collection. Cronies. Network.

Welcome to my company, my clan. ✈

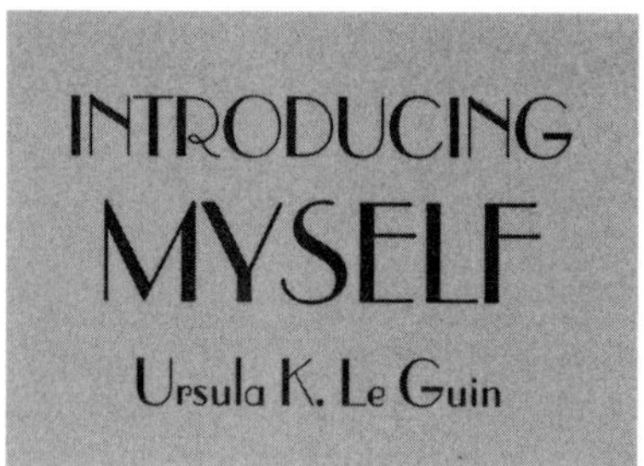

I am a man. Now you may think I've made some kind of silly mistake about gender, or maybe that I'm trying to fool you, because my first name ends in A, and I own three bras, and I've been pregnant five times, and other things like that that you might have noticed, little details. But details don't matter. If we have anything to learn from politicians it's that details don't matter. I am a man, and I want you to believe and accept this as a fact, just as I did for many years.

You see, when I was growing up at the time of the Wars of the Medes and Persians and when I went to college just after the Hundred Years War and when I was bringing up my children during the Korean, Cold, and Vietnam Wars, there were no women. Women are a very recent invention. I predate the invention of women by decades. Well, if you insist on pedantic accuracy, women have been invented several times in widely varying localities, but the inventors just didn't know how to sell the product. Their distribution techniques were rudimentary and their market research was nil, and so of course the concept just didn't get off the ground. Even with a genius behind it an invention has to find its market, and it seemed like for a long time the idea of women just didn't make it to the bottom line. Models like the Austen and the Brontë were too complicated, and people just laughed at the Suffragette, and the Woolf was way too far ahead of its time.

So when I was born there actually were only men. People were men. They all had one pronoun, his pronoun; so that's who I am. I am him, as in "If anybody needs to throw up he will have to do it in his hat," or "A writer knows which side his bread is buttered on ." That's me, the writer, him. I am a man.

Not maybe a first-rate man. I'm perfectly willing to admit that I may be in fact a kind of second-rate or imitation man, a Pretend-a-Him. As a him, I am to a genuine male him as a microwaved fishstick is to a whole grilled Chinook Salmon. I mean, after all, can I inseminate? Can I belong to the Bohemian Club? Can I run General Motors? Theoretically I can, but you know where theory gets us. Not to the top of General Motors, and on the day when a Radcliffe woman is the president of Harvard University you wake me up and

tell me, will you? And then, I can't write my name with pee in the snow. I can't shoot my wife and children and some neighbors and then myself. Oh to tell you the truth I can't even *drive*. I never got my license. I chickened out. I take the bus. That is terrible. I admit it, I am actually a very poor imitation or substitute man, and you can see it when I try to wear those trendy army surplus clothes with ammunition pockets from the Banana Republic Company catalogues and I look like a hen in a pillowcase. I am shaped wrong. People are supposed to be lean, aren't they? You can't be too thin, everybody says so, specially anorexics. People are supposed to be lean, and taut, because that's how men generally are, lean and taut, or anyhow that's how a lot of men start out, and some of them even stay that way. And men are people, people are men, that has been well established; and so people, real people, the right kind of people, are lean. But I'm really lousy at being people, because I'm not lean at all but sort of podgy, with actual fat places. I am untaut. And then, people are supposed to be tough. Tough is good. But I've never been tough. I'm sort of soft and actually sort of tender. Like a good steak. Or like Chinook salmon, which isn't lean or tough, but very rich and tender. But then salmon aren't people, or anyhow we have been told that they aren't, recently. We have been told that there is only one kind of people and they are men. And I think it is very important that we all believe that. It certainly is important to the men.

What it comes down to, I guess, is that I am just not manly. Like Ernest Hemingway was manly. The beard and the guns and the wives and the little short sentences. I do try. I have this sort of beardoid thing that keeps trying to grow, nine or ten hairs on my chin, sometimes even more; but what do I do with the hairs? I tweak them out. Would a man do that? Men don't tweak. Men shave. Anyhow white men shave, and I have even less choice about being white or not than I do about being a man or not. I am white whether I like being white or not. But I do my best not to be, I guess, under the circumstances, because I don't shave. I tweak. But it doesn't mean anything because I don't really have a real beard that amounts to anything. And I don't have a gun and I don't have even one wife and my sentences tend to go on and on and on, with all this syntax in them. Ernest Hemingway would have died rather than have syntax. Or semicolons. I use a whole lot of half-assed semicolons; there was one of them just now; that was a semicolon after semicolons, and another one after 'now.'

And another thing. Ernest Hemingway would have died rather

than get old. And he did. He shot himself. A short sentence. Anything rather than a long sentence, a life sentence. Death sentences are short and very, very manly. Life sentences aren't. They go on and on, all full of syntax and qualifying clauses and confusing references and getting old. And that brings up the real proof of what a mess I have made of being a man: I am not even young. Just about the time they finally started inventing women, I started getting old. And I went right on doing it. I did not stop. I have allowed myself to age and haven't done one single thing about it, with a gun or anything.

What I mean is, if I had any real self respect wouldn't I at least have had a facelift or some liposuction? Although liposuction sounds to me like what they do a lot of on TV when they are young or youngish, though not when they are old, and when one of them is a man and the other is a woman, though not under any other circumstances. What they do is, this young or youngish man and woman take hold of each other and slide their hands around on each other and then they perform liposuction. You are supposed to watch them while they do it. They move their heads around and flatten out their mouth and nose on the other person's mouth and nose and open their mouths in different ways, and you are supposed to feel sort of hot or wet or something as you watch. What I feel is like I was watching two people doing liposuction, and is *this* why they finally invented women? Surely not.

As a matter of fact I think that sex is even more boring, as a spectator sport, than all the other spectator sports, even baseball. I mean, if I have to watch a sport instead of doing it, I'll take show jumping. The horses are really good-looking. The people who ride them are mostly these sort of nazis, but like all nazis they are only as powerful and successful as the horse they are riding, and it is after all the horse who decides whether to jump that five-barred gate or stop short and let the nazi fall off over its neck. Only usually the horse doesn't realize it has the option. Horses aren't awfully bright. But in any case, show jumping and sex have a good deal in common, though you usually can only get show jumping on American TV if you can pick up a Canadian channel. Given the option, though I often forget that I have an option, I certainly would *watch* show jumping and *do* sex. Never the other way round. But I'm too old now for show jumping, and as for sex, who knows? I do; you don't.

Of course golden oldies are supposed to jump from bed to bed these days just like the horses jumping the five-barred gates, bounce,

bounce, bounce, but a good deal of this super sex at seventy business seems to be theory again, like the woman CEO of General Motors and the woman president of Harvard. Theory is invented mostly to reassure people in their forties, mostly men, who are worried. That is why we had Karl Marx, and why we still have economists, though we seem to have lost Karl Marx. As such, theory is dandy. As for practice, or praxis as the Marxists call it apparently because they like x's, you wait till you are sixty or over and then you can tell me about your sexual practice, or praxis, if you want to, though I make no promises that I will listen, and if I do listen I will probably be extremely bored and start looking for some show jumping on the TV. In any case you are not going to hear anything from me about my sexual practice or praxis, now or later.

But all that aside, here I am, old, sixty years old, "a sixty-year-old smiling public man," as Yeats said, but then, he *was* a man. And it's all my own fault. I get born before they invented women, and I live all these decades trying so hard to be a good man that I forget all about staying young, and so I didn't. And my tenses get all mixed up. I just am young and then all of a sudden I was sixty.

There must have been something that a real man could have done about it. Something short of guns, but more effective than Oil of Olay. But I failed. I did nothing. I absolutely failed to stay young. And then I look back on all my strenuous efforts, because I really did try, I tried hard to be a man, to be a good man, and I see how I failed at that. I am at best a bad man. An imitation phony second-rate him with a ten-hair beard and semicolons. And I wonder what was the use. Sometimes I think I might just as well give the whole thing up. Sometimes I think I might just as well exercise my option, stop short in front of the five-barred gate, and let the nazi fall off onto his head. If I'm no good at pretending to be a man and no good at being young, I might just as well start pretending that I am an old woman. I am not sure that anybody has invented old women yet; but it might be worth trying. 

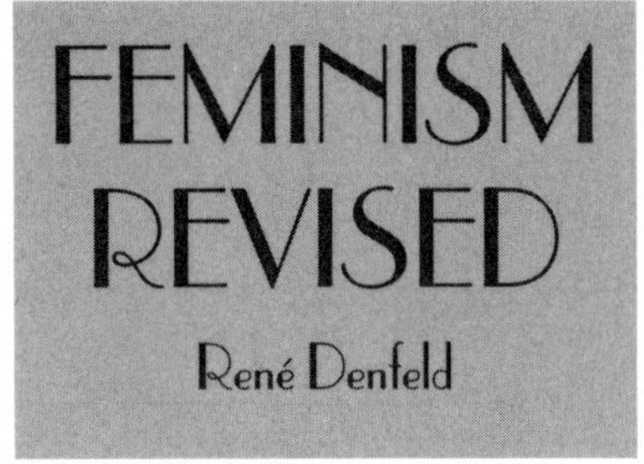

For women of my generation, Betty Friedan's *The Feminine Mystique* was our birth right and Germaine Greer's *The Female Eunuch* our christening gift. The women's movement gave us rights that Friedan, Greer, and our mothers could only dream of, rights that we take as a matter of course. Yet younger women today seem to be moving away from the women's movement. As Susan Faludi points out in her widely respected book *Backlash: the Undeclared War Against Women,* women my age are showing a frightening apathy, if not an open contempt towards feminist activism.

Faludi argues that a backlash driven by "popular culture" is to blame for the distance women of my generation hold the women's movement. The media, she believes, is portraying feminism in a negative light while glorifying the traditional: marriage, motherhood, and home-cooked meals. Younger women are taught, through movies, magazines, and television, to forsake liberation for the joys of home and hearth. While there is a great deal of room to criticize the media's portrayal of feminism, I believe Faludi's argument is flawed by her refusal to address a crucial point — she never once defines what feminism currently stands for. She appears to avoid a question that has been noted elsewhere and begs an answer: what if the problem is the women's movement itself?

I believe it is. As a young woman myself, I feel current feminism has abandoned the struggle for equality, moving into causes that my generation finds foreign, if not repugnant. The women's movement no longer represents my concerns. And it doesn't want to.

I was born in 1967. The previous year saw the founding of the National Organization for Women by Friedan, making headlines in the battle for equal pay, equitable marriage, better education for girls, and political empowerment for women. The year I was born NOW added abortion rights and the equal rights amendment to its platform, and before I was six years old, abortion had been legalized.

While activists such as Friedan gave American women political power with their demands for equal rights, authors such as Greer gave them personal power with their demands for social and sexual freedoms. Women could not be free unless they also owned their sexuality, and so the sexual revolution met the women's movement.

"If you've chosen to be with the man you're with — even if he's the fifth man today," Greer remarked, "if you've chosen him, you are not promiscuous."

By the time I was in grade school, ideas like these — nearly unthinkable in my mother's day — were set. While they may not have always been realities (I vividly remember being called a slut by a boy I made out with when I was eleven or so), the foundation had been laid. Radical changes had occurred: women had joined the work force, were returning to college, choosing careers instead of babies, and enjoying freedoms never before imagined.

For the women my age, belief in equality was never questioned. It existed as a cultural truth. My mother was not the only single hard working parent on the block, and for my brothers, sister, or me to denounce women's rights would have been to denounce her, which was unthinkable. My girlfriends and I played kick-the-can on summer nights, touch football at recess, and sassed back in class. When we strived to get good grades, it was so we could go to college. When we cut classes, it was in order to hang out with friends or even go fishing. At slumber parties, we poured over issues of *Cosmopolitan* ("New Forms of Birth Control: The Pro's and Con's") and talked about sex. We wanted to be veterinarians, jockeys, park rangers, nurses, and millionaires. We decided we wouldn't get married until we were self-sufficient. Or maybe not at all.

We have taken many different paths over the last decade. I left home at sixteen to join a punk band, drank myself silly, and slept with whomever I pleased (birth control and VD check-ups at Planned Parenthood). I supported myself with jobs from dishwashing to physically restraining drunks in Portland's detox center to a short stint as topless dancer. With the money I earned from that job, I took a six month vacation and split to Europe by myself to run around on a motorcycle. I came back a bit calmer and went on to counsel adolescents in an alcohol and drug treatment center, tried bartending, and ended up in my present occupation of freelance writer.

My women friends have also lived their lives as they've pleased. For one friend, that meant moving across the country just because she felt like it. For another, it meant staying home to raise a child. And for a third, it was the full acceptance of her lesbianism. I don't believe I come from a socially protected class (my family is low-income, racially mixed, and lives in North Portland) and yet I don't know any women my age who have felt overly constrained by soci-

etal sexism. I don't know any women who don't believe in their rights. We are feminists.

Without a doubt, society is backpedaling on woman's issues. Twelve years of Republican administrations have made wide inroads into our rights, from attacks on abortion to welfare cuts for single mothers. My friends and I are frightened. It is nearly impossible to think of a society that doesn't have legalized abortion: since we were children, that right has always been a reality. For a generation raised to believe equal opportunity, the Clarence Thomas hearings and President Bush's attacks on NOW were horrifying. And for an age raised during the sexual revolution, Vice President Qualye's condemnation of illegitimate children and their mothers is sickening.

But when we turn to the women's movement, our concerns are not addressed. In fact, they are denounced. It is not enough, it seems, to believe in abortion rights, equal pay, daycare, and equal treatment in the workplace anymore. For many of today's feminists, these are considered subordinate issues. While a few organizations — notably NARAL — remain focused on political reform, the majority of feminists are caught up in movements to ban sexually explicit material, categorize men as inherently violent, and promote a Victorian mindset on female sexuality and identity.

While feminist theorists have explored the issue of pornography for decades, it wasn't until the last few years that the belief that sexually explicit material should be outlawed has gained widespread acceptance within the movement. Robin Morgan, editor of *Ms.* magazine, put the current feminist outlook on porn in a nutshell: "pornography is the theory, and rape is the practice."

I don't buy it, and neither do any of my women friends. Rape existed long before men's magazines and porn shops, and it continues today in countries such as Iran and Saudi Arabia where pornography is not available. To sacrifice our freedom of speech to censor what may or may not cause rape (studies are inconclusive and the variables many) is, for us, contrary to feminism. The women's movement would not exist today if it weren't for the First Amendment.

But the current feminist assumption is that the specter of sexually oriented material must be combated in order for women to be safe. According to Andrea Dworkin, a leader in this movement, "we will not be free until the pornography no longer exists." And so the antiporn movement has come to eclipse other issues. Along with feminist lawyer Catherine MacKinnon, Dworkin has crafted and pushed

several pieces of legislation designed to censor sexually oriented material. One young woman writer questioned these bills succinctly in Portland's *Willamette Week*: If women don't want the government to tell them what to do with their uteruses, why would they want them to tell them what to do with their VCRs?

Morgan and other current feminists believe that there are inherent differences between male and female sexualities. This concept has led to the second major movement in the women's movement; the focus on the pressing problem of male sexuality. Diana Russell, feminist author and contributor to *Ms.* magazine, believes that men have a "propensity" (an intense natural inclination) to rape. In theorizing where this inclination comes from, current feminists have not overlooked the obvious: male genitalia. Dworkin writes that: "Violence is the male; the male is the penis; violence is the penis or the sperm ejaculated from it."

This is Dworkin's male trinity: male/penis/violence. Following this logic, it's not surprising that instead of advocating sexual freedom — as did Greer — current feminists advocate restraint. When the penis becomes violence incarnate, then to play with it becomes tantamount with playing with fire. "[M]ale pleasure is inextricably tied to victimizing, hurting, exploiting," writes Dworkin, "sexual fun and sexual passion…are inseparable from brutality."

I grew up with brothers and have always had male friendships. I could never see my brothers and male friends as inherently violent because they have penises. To me, that is just as sexist as if men saw me as inherently stupid because I have a vagina.

But that seems to be the picture current feminists are painting: If men are dangerous by virtue of their penises, then I, a woman, must be faultless by virtue of my vagina. Violence is a property assigned to the penis; the vagina is pure.

And so current feminists arrive at their third cause: a return to the sexual morality that suffocated my mother's generation. My mother was raised to believe women don't touch themselves while looking at erotic pictures, don't have sex unless they're "safely" married, and don't ever so much as hurt a fly. Primarily, she was taught that women are helpless, incapable of battling the power of men. Today's feminists echo these beliefs. Women are repulsed by sexually explicit material, in danger at all times from all men, and incapable of fighting back. If "violence is the penis or the sperm ejaculated from it," according to Dworkin, then even in his orgasm, the man holds

us captive; he solely owns the property of violence, and thus the power of direct action. As women, we can only be the unwilling receptacles of his trinity.

With the current popularity of the goddess movement within feminism, this return to traditional sexual morality has completed a curiously Victorian idealization of women: not only are they innocents devoid of violence, they are also the salvation of the race. In matriarchal teachings, we are told that women would be much better at running the planet than men, because of our supposed purity and connection to the earth. Men, in true Victorian fashion, are held to be insensitive brutes, unable to control what Dworkin calls their "deep-rooted impulse towards savagery." Women — again in the Victorian tradition — alone have the sensitivity and insight necessary to direct these rampant desires in a more wholesome way. In fact, it is their moral obligation to do so, if only to keep the male sexual organ at a safe distance and maintain the purity of their own genitalia.

A frightening result of this sexual morality in the women's movement is its effect upon activism. In the Victorian age, while women were considered to be property and denied any political rights, there was one social arena where they were allowed to have a voice: the realm of morality. They were, for example, allowed to condemn prostitution and the evils of drink. In today's women's movement, women are allowed to condemn pornography because, in feminist writer Helen E. Longino's words, it is "immoral." But we are discouraged from working within the political system to gain equal rights; first, because the political system is run by men and second, because the greatest danger facing women is the evil of male sexuality, not male dictated law.

Current feminists promote the idea that male sexuality must be transformed and suppressed. Yet the acceptable methods for doing so are constrained by the philosophy behind the goddess movement, which teaches that women can only affect change in society by "visualizing" change within themselves. Consider the feminist anti-pornography movement, which is noteworthy for accomplishing nothing concrete. Even the most politically active members of this movement have failed to pass a single piece of legislation that hasn't been struck down by the courts as unconstitutionally broad.

I won't challenge that this revisionism of old morals is attracting some into the women's movement. It is admittedly appealing: a chance to be the better sex. It is probably as appealing as old boy

sexism is to the boys; to classify and dehumanize half the popula-
tion. But it is the same thing. It is sexism. And within the context of
the current political environment, it is an extremely dangerous move-
ment. Betty Friedan commented succinctly on the effect of the cur-
rent feminist agenda on activism: "A random hatred of men, a ha-
tred that can lead nowhere, with no allies, will produce no signifi-
cant changes; but it will serve as the soil of a fascist appeal."

As a child of the feminist movement, my women friends and I are
baffled and repulsed by the new tenets of feminism. In the real world,
the eradication of sexually explicit material is impossible, and even
if it wasn't, it is doubtful rape would cease. Since many of us have
loved and trusted men, it is nonsense to expect us to judge them by
their genitalia, and in the cases where women do, what does it ac-
complish? I was raised to feel positive about sex, and now current
feminists portray it as redolent with danger, degradation, humilia-
tion, and perversion. And internally, the reaffirmation of a idealized
Victorian woman feels cold and strange to me. I was taught that
women are just as good, *if not the same* as men. My friends and I
believe that there are important rights that include both sexes: free-
dom of speech, freedom from sexism, and freedom to be judged as a
person, not a gender.

Younger women today also believe in other rights: the right to
abortion, equality in the workplace, childcare, equal pay, and equal
opportunity. In discussions with friends my age we confirm these
truths over and over again; we despair of the continuing setbacks
against us.

Susan Faludi is right: younger women today simply aren't joining
the women's movement. When we look towards current feminism,
it is clear our voices are not welcome: "A woman who has *Playboy*
in the house is like a Jew who has *Mein Kampf* on the table," says
feminist activist Judith Bat-Ada, and denounces the sexual revolu-
tion as "breeding a nation of whores."

The women of my age will no more accept this sexually repres-
sive and idealized view of women than we will return to the world
our mothers changed. ح

The day I arrived in Germany was neither sunny nor cloudy, but filled with a swell of noise and confusion that rose and fell like the movements of the ocean. The air was blue-gray from the last thrums of the ship's engines, and the diesel fumes of cargo loaders and nearby locomotives. Coils of cable were bundled near gangways, fell in a maze of lines along the dock, hung from the sides of the ship, hung from the sky itself. Gulls screamed insults, and the tide reeked with the bounty of dead fish, oil, and the debris of ancient shipping lanes. Only the ocean smell of salt saved us from a foulness that would have been unbearable.

It was the grandest sight I'd ever imagined. I was not yet eighteen, and my mother had just given me the ultimate reprieve: a ticket to some place miles away from her house. And not just any place, but one full of the glitter and sparkle of unfamiliar words, curlicues and inflections of French, German, Portuguese, Greek, and a symphony of other languages. That day at the dockside in Bremerhaven, I plunged into a world of new sounds without any notion of what was expected of me, a St. Louis colored girl, wide-eyed and trying to look cool. Aside from the rumors of entertainers who had left the States, and West Indians who showed up at weddings and family reunions, I'd had no close contact with black folks who spoke something other than English. Moreover, I had "the butcher's ear" — *L'oreille du boucher,* or *der Hörerschlächter.*

As far as I know, my grandmother coined that term. It was her way of describing the butcher's reluctance to follow her instructions regarding which cut of meat she wanted him to prepare. In those days, when I lived with her while my father was off to war and my mother worked to supplement her WWII army allotment, neighborhoods were segregated, and butchers sent the choicest cuts of meat to the white side of town. My grandmother took me with her if she had to talk to the butcher. But no matter how many ration stamps or how precise her descriptions and my reinforcements, the butcher translated our order as a request for the fatty end, the bony cut, the gristle, as if he had suddenly grown deaf. And so for my grand-

mother, to be deaf, to not hear what you were told to do, was to own the butcher's ear. If I forgot an errand or did my chores haphazardly, she accused me of having the butcher's ear. If I continued to play a game of stick ball or sweet-rosie-in-the-cornfield instead of coming home as soon as she called to me, she would claim my good sense surely had been possessed by the butcher's ear.

"Chile, what's the matter with you?" she'd say. "You act like you can't listen to me no better than that butcher."

I may not have been totally possessed by the butcher's ear in my youth, but I certainly came to acknowledge its presence later whenever I attempted to speak a foreign language. I have, in the course of some forty years of travels, heard languages with an ear trained on the Mason-Dixon line, the mythical gateway to the West, the border state — Missouri. Not exactly Southern but certainly not Northern, my speech was as confined to region as those cuts of meat the butcher foisted off on my grandmother — the sounds of language dulled by the limitations of monolinguistic culture, and tempered by dialect, often leading me down dangerous paths where I wander, like some luckless tourist, lost in a Casbah of extra syllables and wayward sounds.

When I arrived in Germany in 1953, I was bound for the University, equipped with a Missouri accent and a pocketful of textbook phrases. My mother doggedly pulled us through Customs, where she managed the maze of redtape as long as we were confronted with U.S. personnel, most of whom carried the same drawl of sounds she had been accustomed to hearing in the States. Once we left dockside, she deposited me on a train for Munich.

The last English I would hear for a while was my mother saying, "I want you to take care-ah of y'rself, you hear-ah?"

I waved my mother a cheery good-bye and looked down the length of the train. For a moment, I imagined I had stumbled into one of the movies I'd seen during Saturday matinees at the Antioch Theater near my grandmother's house. That train was a relic out of films where spies lurked in corridors and spoke the language of espionage, the kind of conversations found in movies starring actors like Claude Rains, Adolf Menjou, Una Merkel, Charles Boyer, or Marlene Dietrich. When we got underway, each whistle's shriek, and clatter of wheels brought me back to those matinees at the Antioch theater.

And that train ride was my first real encounter with another lan-

guage. Any other contacts had been confined to classroom imitation and rote. Given the opportunity, I could say, without hesitation, in French or in German, "The teacher is at the blackboard," or "The book is on the table." (To this day, I have not had to use either of those phrases in real life.) But in those days, I was a dutiful student, and memorized whatever was required of me. I settled into my train compartment and tried to look suave — *suavè*, I whispered, convinced a word so full of worldliness needed an accented ending. As the train sped through the German countryside, moving away from the gray hillsides of mining towns into vineyards and farms linked by thick patches of woods, I opened my map and read aloud the names of places that tracked the route to Munich.

"Düsseldorf," I began. "Kaiserslautern. Tübingen. Ulm," trying to slide past glottal stops without swallowing my tongue.

"Du bist eine Amerikanerin?" a woman seated across from me asked.

"Yeah... uh... Ja," I said, recovering quickly. "Studenta," I said, aiming for a word that was vaguely German at least.

The woman seemed to not notice my efforts. "Willkommen ans Deutschland," she smiled.

"Dun-ker shine, mayan Frau-ah," I slowly answered, decorating each word with Missouri

"Jawohl," she laughed. "Willkommen."

I had begun my first conversation. Sure, it was a poor beginning, but remember: I had the butcher's ear, one trained in a land plowed flat as an altar board, flooded each spring by the mighty Mississippi River and pocketed with hidden caves. Language was merely another detail on an unforgiving landscape, one to be mastered with an ear that had been trained to hear only certain sounds. Geography marked the speech of both blacks and whites. Vowels were heard as gulps of sound flipping through the air of consonants, and the consonants themselves sometimes falling short of finding their places in words. So I know I'm not too far from home when I hear someone say *pen* so that it sounds like *pin*, or *celery* equals *salary*, while "Little *aw'fun* Annie *aw'fun* goes to the store," and *Washington* becomes *Warshin'ton*. I can conjure up memories of St. Louis, whether I hear these sounds from a redheaded flight attendant who tries to reassure me when midwestern weather creates death-defying airpockets, or from my mother, who is convinced that my obsession with traveling will be the death of me yet. Whoever the speaker, I know we have been trained with the same ear.

My strange meanderings through foreign languages began with that first trip to Europe where I learned to breathe in the sounds of other languages, all the cacophonies and glides, the hums, clicks, and hisses that unravel into an abundance of new words holding lives so clearly unlike mine, yet somehow, very familiar. In this country, I had not been expected to learn another language, and was in fact, suspected of not really knowing English. Stateside education had not prepared me for the likes of Alexander Dumas, Leopold Senghor, or Aimé Césaire. I'd only heard about two kinds of black folks — those in Africa and those in America. (Speaking the Spanish of Central America and the Caribbean was not enough to place anyone of color outside of those categories, and African languages were depicted as a gumbo mixture of grunts and gestures straight from Hollywood.)

But although I now can say my world has expanded beyond the limits of textbook rituals, in truth, I began practicing for other languages when I was living with my grandmother.

An only child, I was stuck in my grandmother's house through snowy St. Louis winters, and entertained myself with a wind-up Victrola and a box of old phonograph records. My companion had been a 1920s boudoir mirror — silver-plated and wooden framed, crowned with a finial that curled like a lady's hairdo. In front of that mirror, I plotted my invasion of the world with all the wonderful Blues ladies of 78 rpm records. I mimicked adult conversations, not knowing exactly what words to use but aiming for the intonation and nuance of utterances. What I did not hear, I approximated. With my butcher's ear, I could not always distinguish where one word ended and another began, so I relied on the weft and warp of inflection. Valaida Snow and I discussed how she'd come to own a golden trumpet. "Child, don't you know I got it in the Netherlands?" she said, with a hint of French, or was it Russian, in her voice. And I answered in my own made-up tongue, shrugging my shoulders and sashaying to the beat of Valaida's all-girl band. When Josephine Baker fell under the command of my grandmother's Victrola needle, I threw an old feather boa around my shoulders and imagined myself in Le Beau-Chêne, resting after a round of supper clubs. I heard only the words that rhymed, but I could trill R's, and *mon, ton, bon,* right along with Josephine.

"Don't you go acting like Josephine Baker," the women in my family would say. "Took herself over to Europe and didn't come

back. No telling what went on over there."

So naturally, I paid special attention to Josephine's songs. What better teacher than a black woman who had defied convention, who could set my pulse racing on a tremolo of accented and circumflected sounds? I strained to hear the words and mimicked what she sang. But it would take more than Josephine to help me wrestle with the butcher's ear.

"All you have to do is try," American friends said, although they giggled in amazement at what happened to German under the influence of Southern speech. Still I tried, *dun-ker shining* and *wheater-sayun* my way from phrase to phrase, and surprisingly, I quickly found a circle of friends, German or others, who expected me to speak their language. In fact, in Europe I discovered language was not color exclusive. For the first time, being black was not a line that would separate me from other languages. For the first time, I had as much trouble with being identified as an English-speaking American as I had with someone's reaction to the color of my skin.

My best German lessons began when I met Wilma Hessel. Winter was a slate-gray sky cast over classrooms, Gasthauses, side streets, and little parks with twig bent trees. I had come to the park because it was important to get away from American students. When I was with them, all the Germans I met wanted to practice English. Wilma had no such intentions. German or English, it was a trade off for her. She was a "brown baby," not from World War II, but from between the Wars when her mother, a singer, had met her father, a bistro owner.

"There some of us everywhere," my grandmother had told me. "Don't need to look for 'em. They find you."

Wilma Hessel had found me — or I had found her — by accident one afternoon on the bridge near the Deutsches Museum. I was watching German families strolling past, and fat little kids in lederhosen scatter birds trying to eat the few seeds sprinkled on the ground. The leaves were rustling like the sound of nylon stockings brushing together under a woman's skirts, and the sun had bronzed everything.

"Ich bein eine Deutschen," Wilma had said.

The words did not ring true until I understood how I identified myself as American first, black second. "Ich bein eine Amerikanerin, "I said. "Negro," I added, as if that were necessary.

Wilma placed her hand over mine. Our hands together, one light brown, one dark brown, were not very different. "Amerikanerin," Wilma said. "Und Deutschen." When she looked at me, there was laughter in her eyes. I joined her, and we both laughed, knowing how little we actually had said with those words. It is what happens when words betray you, when they hide what you truly want to say.

Wilma became my anchor, my touchstone with reality in a time that still seems to me unreal. But she was genuine, an in-the-flesh, bonafide motorcycle mama. Her only problem was that there were damned few motorcycles in postwar Germany. So Wilma was stuck with a motor scooter, a Vespa painted jazzy yellow, with a windscreen curved like a VW hood. We zipped past VWs, around 1930s Ford trucks, putt-putts that seemed to run on sheer willpower alone. Wilma especially liked to take on old cars, revving the Vespa engine when we pulled along side sedans with running boards and high windows that looked like they'd been pulled off the back lot of a Claude Rains movie — "Third Reichers," she called them.

We sped down streets that had been swept cleaner than any place I'd ever been. And not just swept, but picked clean until every dust-pan full of gravel, every brick, door, or windowpane was accounted for as the country went about the business of coming to life after decades of horror. Most streets held the ruins of some building, an archway guarding an upheaval of bricks, the shell of a house hidden behind a scarred wall on which politicians' flyers announcing the re-birth of West Germany had been posted.

Munich 1953 was no different from Köln, Düsseldorf, Frankfurt, or other cities. Rebuilding went on along side the obvious traces of Hitler's disaster — the ruined spires of Frauenkirche looming above a ragged skyline, scaffolding hugging the fire-blackened skeleton of the opera house near the Hofgarten, and from the upheaval of cobblestones banked on either side of Marionplatz, the niches of the Glockenspiel, gaunt and empty of the clock's guardians. Two blocks away, a new building stood like a messenger out of the future.

"Nein, nein... Go right! Rechts! Rechts! Schnell!," Wilma would yell as I swerved to avoid a VW, a Mercedes, or a lorry. My greatest fear was the trolley car, old wooden trams with unpredictable brakes, and drivers who plowed through traffic with a vengeance. The Strassenbahn bell was like a ten second warning. Those who dared, took the outside lanes, where the rush of oncoming traffic and nar-

row streets was not unlike riding the downhill loop on a roller coaster. I still can swear better in German than in any other foreign language, perhaps because I learned those phrases when death was barreling toward me in the form of a Strassenbahn, its seats removed for firewood, and a maniac at the wheel.

I kept confusing my right with my left, so whenever I signaled a turn, I looked like I was waving off the fertilizer smells of some invisible honey wagon. Wilma would yell, "Vamanos! Vamanos!" as if I weren't going fast enough already. Except when Wilma said, "Vamanos, " it sounded more like: "Vomiting! Vomiting!" so I didn't know whether to stop or pick up speed. I think I may have wanted time to stop, to capture the two of us forever, in our leather jackets, pedal pushers, saddle shoes, and sunglasses, scooting down the highway, singing, "Hey bop-o-rebop," as if we were practicing for Ted Mack's Amateur Hour.

Some afternoons, Wilma and I would sit with friends in outdoor cafes, drinking beer and smoking contraband cigarettes, the raw burnt-leather smell of local tobacco mingling with the smoke from Camels and Viceroys. Our companions were German, French, Italian, Senegalese, Turkish, and a few, I suspected, whose papers were not in order, as Claude Rains invariably would say before the spy movie ended.

Evenings we'd head for the Hofbrauhaus for bockbeer and fat sausages, or to a club in Schwabing to see someone like Jeanne Marcelle (billed as: Der Fisch and Ihrer Angel). But in that cafe crowd of artists, poets, students, and drifters at the Tabu or Atelier, no one asked for official papers. In fact, by tacit agreement, we had a great disdain for anything official. We argued the merits of life where all rules were broken. And when the talk turned to heritage, confusing color and race, as I had been taught to do back home, did not let me off the hook. I was expected to carry my weight in the conversation, and was asked to explain what I meant when I said I was a "Negro," or had African roots. It was the first time I'd been asked those questions, and I began to understand how, in a world that could be turned inside-out and upside-down, color was too simple and American too misleading.

I began by looking at who we were. We represented a hodge-podge of races, a sort of impromptu version of Josephine Baker's adopted "Rainbow Tribe," but more loose-knit. We played at being

family the way I remembered playing "let's pretend" games in grade
school, when younger kids who had no siblings claimed an older
playmate to give them status in the schoolyard. There was Siglinde,
who spent far too much time trying to explain how young Germans
had been sucked into defending the Vaterland. And Stein Eric, whose
family had fled both the Italian and German armies, and whose
brother had been killed fighting with the Vichy French. And Lily, who
remembered the war as the crackle of a radio constantly attended by
her family at their farmhouse in Wales. And Dedes, who saw his first
black American when soldiers landed near his village in Morocco.
"They were black, like me, but I could not understand why they did
not speak French, " he said. And Claudette Gèrard and Mike
Tushman and all the others who swore we'd keep in touch, forever,
even while the world went to hell in a handbasket, as we knew it
some day would. We were fatalists, but by the same token, we
thought we were invincible. (Perhaps that is the way I can explain
challenging fate on a motor scooter.) I only know that when a hand-
some suitor insisted on drinking a stein of the Hofbrau's finest beer
from my slipper, I swear I heard Josephine laughing along with me
as I limped home in a soggy shoe.

Despite my bobby socks, angora sweaters, and poodle skirts, Josephine
Baker was certainly with me on my first visit to Europe. But where
she had found the highlife of Paris and Berlin, I mostly saw the ordi-
nary days of Bavaria, days punctuated with the hunger of post-war
Germany, and the unsettling beauty of Black Forest country.

Unlike Josephine Baker, I could not say *j'ai deux amours*. The only
love I developed was a romance of possibilities, the love of travel.
My first trip abroad was a journey into a fairy tale land of ginger-
bread houses, eiderdown beds, gabled rooftops and chimney pots
hiding a maelstrom of incongruities. But it was a step away from the
U.S., and I no longer had to rely on my memory of Adolf Menjou
and matinees at the Antioch.

My travels have become my own stories of adventure. Six months,
three months, three weeks — I take my leave of the world I know in
order to step, for a moment, into other worlds where play sisters
await, bright with stories. I still blunder into languages other than
English with the awe I had when I first listened to Josephine Baker
on my grandmother's Victrola, but now, more than ever, I try to shed
the butcher' s ear.

By my second year in Germany, I was living on the economy, working as an *au pair* girl and going to school part-time. I began to frequent a butcher shop near my flat on Hansa Allee. Unlike St. Louis, that butcher shop presented another kind of trap. No purchase was simple. In exchange for an exorbitant number of Deutschmarks, I had to listen to the butcher's stories about the old days — "When the King was Prussian," he would boast. He had a line up of pictures on the wall — idyllic settings with castles and the remains of castles scattered throughout Germany, near Nymphenburg, Grunwald, Friedberg, and a score of other places I can't remember. Each time I went to the store, I received another story about the castles.

"After the war, not so many," he'd say. "Nicht sehr viele." But no matter how much he talked, he always sliced a choice piece of schnitzel or pork cut according to my request.

"They are beautiful," I'd tell him. "Ja, Schönheit. Sehr gut," I'd say, and watch the butcher turn to me, smiling.

I'd smile back. We had spoken to each other, the butcher and I. So I shifted my singular rucksack of English and midwestern sounds, and made do, as my grandmother would have advised. ⌒

PHOTO ESSAY

Marsha Burns

M arsha Burns was born in 1945 and lives in Seattle, Washington. She is known for both her commercial and artistic photographic work. Photographing individuals who she encounters on the streets, Burns shows a concern for the gestures and accoutrements that define a person. In this series of seven black and white portraits, street youth from Frankfurt, Germany, and New York City watch us watching them.

Anita, Frankfurt, 1987

Mola, Frankfurt, 1987

Oliver, Frankfurt, 1987

Muthe, Frankfurt, 1987

Kassa, New York, 1986

Raphella, New York 1986

Marietta & Peter, Frankfurt, 1987

José Maria Alberny was the son of the butcher. He was older than the gang he hung out with in the early sixties in Figueras, an hour or two north of Barcelona: the band of young men of which I — a girl, nineteen years old — became an honorary member. I didn't exactly become "one of the boys" — I was always obviously different. Though most of them were about my age or a couple of years older, how could I fail to be different at six feet tall, towering over all of them except Alberny, who was my height if I took off my shoes? And there was my blond hair, bleached almost white by salt and sun. The boys were all so dark with their olive skins and black hair — all, that is, except for Jaime, whose medium brown hair and bluish eyes won him the nickname of "Jaime El Rubio," though in most company from the northern climes he would have been just a nondescript darkish-haired boy.

No, I was hardly one of the boys, although I was admitted to the group as no other female was. Spanish girls were not available. They didn't get to go out alone, much less sit in cafes after dinner drinking coffee and cognac. They couldn't pile into someone's car with the gang, heading for one of the local village fiestas. Spanish girls appeared together in groups, walking arm in arm up and down the rambla before dinner. One or two of them were engaged to boys in Alberny's gang, but I never saw the happy couples together. As for foreign girls, they were simply prey — especially the blonds: legitimate targets, the boys thought, for their macho exhibitionism. The difference between those girls and me was that they all hung out at the beach, where they rented apartments, hotel rooms, or boarded at pensions for two or three weeks, whereas I lived in Figueras, the only foreigner for much of the summer, and certainly the only single, foreign female. Somehow my proximity — my appearance in the cafe at breakfast time and after dinner, my frequent shopping trips at the weekly market, and my regular appointments with Alberny's aunt-by-marriage, the hairdresser in Calle Gerona — put me outside the category of legitimate prey. To pursue for-

eign girls required a trip to the artificial world of beach resorts and nightclubs: a trip far away from this very traditional world. I was too close to home — almost family, or at least an honorary townsgirl: a girl whose reputation needed protection, even though I myself clearly showed no respect for proper behavior. Night after night, I scandalized the population of Figueras by roaring back from the beach at three or four in the morning in my little sports car. But day after day, I lived among them, shopping and gossiping like anybody else, and, perhaps because I didn't yet know enough to act guilty or evasive about the nocturnal adventures, they rallied around me as they would have rallied around a wayward daughter of the town. In fact, looking back on it now, I think they were, in some mysterious way, proud of my independence — proud to allow me, by virtue of my foreignness, the freedom none of them could claim.

I spent most of my time with all the boys together. Pedro's father would sometimes lend us his taxi for a group outing, while three or four more could pile into my little open M.G., with a couple sitting up precariously on the back. This was how we traveled to the fiesta at San Pablo de la Roca — my first experience of a village fiesta. As we bumped into the village over cobbles liberally sprinkled with mule dung, my passengers lurched and shouted with excitement. The crisp roar of our exhaust echoed between the ancient walls of the monastery and the old town fortifications, as people jumped aside shouting "*Carrumba!*" and whistling at our festive appearance. Over the next three hours, I won a purple rabbit for shooting a hole in a plastic egg, danced three *sardanas*, towering over the circle of precise dancers, barely escaped throwing up in the swingboats, and was stared at long and hard by everybody in the crowd (to which I was perfectly accustomed by this time).

On another occasion, at the height of summer's heat, we drove in procession to the lake at Bañolas, where the world water-ski championships were being held. We lounged in the shade of weeping willow trees, reveling in the unfamiliar coolness of the mountain air and eating *tortillas españolas* pressed between huge hunks of fresh bread, while the speedboats roared up and down the lake, and the skiers, like Canadian geese in early fall, swooped hither and thither, taking off from ramps, soaring and skimming, and, once in a while, plunging clumsily into the water with ill-timed excitement. As the afternoon turned to dusk, we clowned in front of someone's

camera, producing a few overexposed snapshots which I still have somewhere in the bottom of a drawer.

There were times, however, when I would abandon the group and go out on a date with one or other of the boys. Jaime El Rubio took me to Granny's Nightclub in Rosas, Isidro took me to dinner at the Camping Pous, where he taught me to drink from a *purrón* and I poured red wine all down the front of my dress, and José Serra took me to a dinner dance at the very fancy Hotel Cap Sa Sal at Aigua Blava, where they once filmed a James Bond movie. Looking back on it, I wonder how much these dates had to do with the M.G., which all the boys worshipped unreservedly, and how much with me. Anyway, regardless of the car appeal, I suspect the group had an agreement about me — maybe one that Alberny had created and enforced. In marked contrast to virtually every other date during my three years in Spain, none of the gang ever tried anything sexual with me. They very properly escorted me home to my door and shook my hand, or once in a while offered a chaste kiss on the cheek. Again I was getting treated like a girl who lived among them might be treated — though of course she might never be allowed to go on the date in the first place.

The two dates I had with Alberny himself were different. While the other boys acted as if I were someone's sister or a strange cousin visiting from afar, who should be given a good time but treated as family, Alberny, having instigated this policy, clearly had the option of abandoning it if he chose — and sometimes he seemed close to doing so. His power fascinated me. It was probably what made him the only one in the group I found attractive. I have tried to remember if I acted seductive when we were alone, but that time is hard to conjure up, perhaps because I had no self-awareness. I did not analyze what was happening, but lived from day to day, recording in my small diary only the bare facts: "went to Cap Sa Sal with J.M. Danced till 2" or "Drinks with the gang. Alberny left early."

I certainly felt intensely intimate with Alberny that day we watched the sunset from the highest hill in the park outside town, sitting on a bed of aromatic pine needles, the light melting away into a solid black wall of cicada song. I might well have been afraid, even angry, if he had succeeded in putting aside his obvious conflict and grabbed me, but the truth was I liked his visible conflict. I liked his moody, foreboding silences, during which I deduced, as perhaps he meant me to, that he was virtuously grappling with an

overwhelming desire to kiss me. I liked his "big brother" protective stance, mixed with the dangerous possibilities that lurked in his too-intense gaze. I liked his slicked-back hair and his black jeans and his attention.

Alberny was uneducated, arrogant, and full of the prejudices common to Catalans at that time but, even after what happened later, I couldn't write him off as a mean person. He had excessive amounts of certain Spanish male traits — a reverence for his mother and mothers in general, an impatient desire to have children, and an intense pride in who he was and in his people. "His people" included family, all the townsfolk (except guardias and those shadowy figures who had become rich by throwing in their lot with Franco in '36), and all Catalans. They also included the English, the Dutch, and the Americans, many of whom he went out of his way to meet as they passed through Figueras, setting himself up as a kind of host and town guide, though he spoke no English. He would lead whole families to the cafe, sit down with them and order them San Miguel beers or cognacs, which he would refuse to let them pay for. When they remonstrated, he would wave his hand graciously and tell them in Catalan that such a thing was unthinkable. "His people," however, did not stretch to include the Italians, the Germans, the French, or Spaniards from Andalucía, these last of whom he considered an embarrassment to the country because of their poverty, their short stature, and their "uneducated" speech. Perhaps it was Alberny's pride, or some (to me) mysterious aspect of his machismo, that led to what happened that Thursday night in August, though I'm not at all sure about his motivation, and even less sure about my own.

We were all sitting outside the cafe — perhaps ten of us at a table right next to the curb. Trucks rattled past, blowing out billows of noxious exhaust and drowning out pieces of the conversation. It was about ten or ten-thirty in the evening and our group was still expanding as the boys wandered out from their mothers' dinner tables. I sat next to Alberny, who dominated the group with his particular intensity and by virtue of being the oldest. Jaime El Rubio was there. So was Francisco who worked at the *farmacia*. Isidro sat silent behind his round wire-rim glasses, which had led me to mistake him for an intellectual when I first saw him. Blanc smiled at me and offered cigarettes. They all talked very fast in Catalan but whenever anyone addressed me directly, he switched to

Castilian. Even my presence and their good manners, however, could not hold them to a language which was so much less familiar, and certainly less beloved, than the Catalan they grew up with.

Soon the conversation started to revolve around me: my independence; my ability to live alone, travel alone, drive a fast car, stay out dancing until dawn, and generally do whatever I wanted without consulting anyone, or waiting around for invitations. The boys were not deterred by my embarrassment. "She's tough," someone said, with admiration. "Yes, tough like a boy," agreed someone else. But Alberny demurred. "She's a girl," he said flatly. "No girl is tough like a boy," and his dark eyes turned to me with a challenge.

There was a moment's silence. Though I certainly didn't think about it at the time, I now see that I was meant to agree: to giggle like a girl, maybe to argue ineffectively and defer to his masculinity. I suppose this was just one of several openings he created through which I could have embarked upon a spectacular but doomed affair. But I never saw the possibility — at least, not on those terms. I didn't have it in me to giggle and assent to the assumption of my feminine weakness.

"She's tough, is she?" Alberny said mockingly, his eyes never leaving mine as he scraped his chair up close and took a drag of his black-tobacco cigarette, leaving it between his lips while the strong-smelling smoke wound up in front of his eyes and around his greased-back cowlick. "I don't think she's so very tough, you know." And he smiled at me, at first gently, and then with the full force of his charm and male arrogance.

Still I remained silent. Slowly he brought up his hand and removed the cigarette. Slowly he lowered his hand with the cigarette between his thumb and forefinger till he was holding it, glowing tip down, a few inches above the back of my right hand, which was resting on the white iron table. "No," he said, still smiling. "She doesn't like to get hurt. She's just like all the girls."

This was another opening for me. I could still giggle and defer, but again I did not understand. These rituals had somehow escaped my education and, to this day, I can't explain why. Most of my friends had learned how to play this game with boys, but I had always stubbornly, and painfully, held back. So instead of grabbing his wrist and laughingly agreeing with him — instead of a coy "Oh, José Maria, of course I don't like to get hurt!"— I simply stared back at him. I dare say there was as much challenge in my stare as

in his, as our gazes interlocked like the interlocking of two arm wrestlers' hands. It was a decisive moment. The joke evaporated and something serious was afoot.

All the boys fell silent. The traffic kept up its din, but our table sat as if in its own protected bubble of quietness. Arturo, the waiter, stopped clearing a nearby table and froze, his tray held high, as Alberny's cigarette came closer and closer to the back of my hand. Alberny's fingers were shaking very slightly and the dark smoke continued to spiral its way up into the large sunshade that covered the table, gathering in a murky pocket under the words *Martini Blanco,* that showed red through the white canvas. Then I could feel the warmth approach my skin. Alberny's eyes seemed to flash. His mouth curved a little as he waited for me to jerk back my hand and jump up. The joke could still work and he believed it would. But still I stared into his eyes. I saw him hesitate. I saw his eyes glance quickly towards my hand, checking out how close the glowing cigarette was to my tanned skin. And then I saw his inability to back down.

Alberny set his lips in a grim expression that would probably become a permanent part of his middle-aged face, and moved the cigarette down. I never moved. Never flinched — not at the first touch and not as the pain set in. There was a smell of burning flesh and there were tears in my eyes, but they did not overflow and I did not move a muscle as I continued to stare into Alberny's eyes. After what seemed like a very long time — but might actually have been five or ten seconds — he looked down at my hand, removed the cigarette and tossed it into the street. "Wait here," he said in a matter-of-fact tone, "I'll get you something for it." As he walked away from the cafe, his shoulders drooped just a little.

The boys started talking again. Blanc put an arm around my shoulder and asked if I was OK, while Arturo started to clatter his cups and spoons. I nodded and breathed — then breathed some more, concentrating on not feeling anything beyond the intense pain on my right hand, until Alberny returned with antiseptic ointment and Band-Aids. Very gently he dressed the small round wound, which was quite deep and throbbing now. When he was done, he smiled at me — a smile of complicity with no challenge left in it — and ordered a brandy for me. Maybe it was then, or maybe a day or so later, when I continued to appear with the wound covered, that he said, "So, I've made my mark on you, haven't I?"

I don't remember anything else about that night: how I left or at what time. Nor do I remember how long the burn took to heal. All I know is that Alberny treated me differently after that. I might have been his sister — not a little sister, but one the same age as him or older. He was still protective, but now there was unambiguous respect. His conflict was gone, the door to passion closed forever: our relationship and something important about the rest of my life both decided. 

FOOD FOR THE DEAD

Kathleen Tyau

Gold and silver paper money burns next to bowls of sun-warmed dumplings and rice, once soft, now hardening in the April wind. We have come to the cemetery with my grandmother to *bai san,* pray for our dead grandfather and bring him food, whiskey, and money. Popo lights red candles with the smoking punk stick. Last night we folded many pieces of paper money, which Popo sends to Goong Goong by fire so he will have lots of money to buy houses and clothes in heaven. She wails softly in a sing-song voice and presses her palms together and bows towards the grave. I crawl into the circle of her arms and bow with her hands covering mine. Three times I bow, and then my cousins take their turns. I play around the gravesite while the others pray.

Don't step on Goong Goong's head. If you step on his head, he will think you do not honor him.

I tiptoe around the concrete border of the grave, careful not to touch the grass, holding my breath and crossing my fingers when I slip.

Mama, tell me about Goong Goong.

He tied your feet to the high chair because you made so much noise while you were eating. You kicked and screamed. Your grandfather was the only one who could stop you from crying at the table. He looked like a beach boy. He lifted weights. He owned a store in Waikiki and used the money to buy land. If he had lived long enough, you would be rich. We would be rich. But he got sick. He had a bad cough. The doctors thought he had pneumonia, but two months later he died of lung cancer. And you wouldn't stop crying. You cried so much, I had to stay home from his funeral. So, don't step on Goong Goong's head. We'll go home soon and you can eat.

We pour the whiskey and tea on the grass and carry the bowls of food back to the car. Back at home, everyone sits down at the long table to eat. Lumps of meat bulge through the translucent skin of the dumplings, and the noodles feel slippery, like the brains I crawled on in the spook house at Halloween. I close my eyes and try to see my Goong Goong smiling, holding me high in the sky, running with me on the beach. But all I see are flesh and brains, charred skin floating into the sky, spirits rising from the grave. I hear my grandmother, my mother, my whole family wailing. I want to kick my chair and scream. ✍

The day JFK was shot you laid me in the mud
and ground the boy-doll into me.
But even Ken could not commit the sin
of trespass, his organ palsied in a lump.
Child: you were breeding new America
from my petrochemical body, my breasts
two warheads aimed at Cuba, right buttock
bearing the mark of a toy empire.

You found my seams all shut: price
paid for deathless crotch, for afternoons
spent wheeling round the yard in the Dreamobile.
The Johnson years, you left me
locked for days in a vinyl coffin full of gowns.
My feet were arched in ready spasm
for those tiny spiked heels
you'd have me grind into a rival's commie eye.

By the time Bobby fell in Tinseltown,
you'd cropped my hair in tufts and scattered
all my haute couture to rain and mud.
I shuffled naked, like girls in crazywards
searching magazines for their lost faces.
And when you find your parents dead — and they
        will die —
you'll find me buried in their basement
and wonder why you mackled me with ink tat-
        toos.

Think then where your memory begins:
running home, lunchbox taking chinks out of
        your thigh,
to find your mother weeping in the kitchen,
her radio full of ghosts. Remember
how it was me, not her, you chose to comfort,
how I was dressed in pillbox pink and brought
        outside
to play Dallas's First Lady against a hero's effigy.
How his perfect body rained in pieces on my skin.

BARBIE Tells Her BIOGRAPHY

Lucia Maria
Perillo

CLOCK PUNCHERS

David James Duncan

It's Sabbath afternoon. Papa and me are sitting in the papermill parking lot, waiting for his friend Roy to get off work. Roy was supposed to be through at 3 o'clock, but the mill clock says 3:14, and nobody argues with the mill clock: its hour hand alone is half the size of a telephone pole.

Back in 1960 — not long after Papa lost the lawsuit that could have fixed his dead thumb — Jan Lacey, the guy who cleans the pigeon shit off the mill clock's numbers, fell backwards out of the 0 in the 10 when a yellow jacket stung him. It was lunch hour, I guess, because a bunch of people saw it happen. They said he did a slow, sloppy backflip but landed right side up on the asphalt, neat as you please, right between two parked cars. He broke his pelvis, as I remember, and several bones in his legs and feet, but was healthy enough to be on the TV news later the same evening, so we all gathered round to watch. They showed the huge, high clock first, then panned slowly down the concrete wall to the place where Lacey landed. Next they took you right up to his hospital room, where he lay grinning at the bright lights and camera despite the casts and pulleys and cables holding all his broken parts in place. The TV news lady came up with a pretty good question for a change. "What were your exact thoughts, Mr. Lacey," she said, "what flashed through your mind as you plummeted down toward what must have seemed like certain death?"

While the camera slid in for a close-up, Jan screwed his face up and thought hard about it. He thought for several seconds — which seemed like an awful lot of thinking for somebody on TV. Then he said, "Oopseedaisy."

The news lady cocked her head, obviously not understanding. "Yep," Lacey said, all solemn and nodding. "Oopseedaisy. Those was my very words."

We all found this funny, and laughed pretty hard. But when Pap heard it he almost died. I mean he writhed and howled in his chair till the tears streamed and his face and stomach cramped and he started coughing and choking. Then he caught his breath and started

in all over again. All that evening, clear to bedtime, all any of us had to do was whisper "Oopseedasiy" and he would lose it again. I remember his whooping, his writhing, his wet, helpless face. I remember it all perfectly. I remember it because he hasn't laughed once since.

…

There's nothing in sight but the mill clock, but you can actually watch time pass on this clock, so that's what I do: I watch the tip of the phone pole-sized aluminum minute hand glide across the concrete face of the building. I remember Irwin once saying that he liked the mill clock because it made a person stop and think. And I remember Everett replying that it made you think all right: it made you think it might not be a bad idea to go buy yourself a big ol' horse pistol and blow your brains out. I don't feel quite like blowing my brains out, but when I try for a while to move my hand as slowly and steadily as the mill clock's hand is moving, it's sure not fun. The human mind and body just aren't built for anything so slow and boring. If Father Time has a brain, I'll bet it's about the size of a BB.

I guess what the mill clock makes me stop and think about is the Aesop fable of the tortoise and the hare. The clock seems like the victorious tortoise, and the men filing in and out of the mill seem like the stupid speedy hares. I've always hated Aesop's stories. Especially the little punchlines at the end where he plays preacher and tells you what everything supposedly means. If Aesop was alive today I'll bet he'd be writing yarns for *Pathfinder Magazine*, calling things like "Why Tommy Tortoise Told Satan No." I'll bet Aesop's brain wasn't much bigger than Father Time's. I wish there really was such a thing as a Time-Clock Puncher, though. I wish some gigantic, surly, stone-fisted guy went wandering around the world smashing every clock in sight till there weren't any more and people got so confused about when to go to the mill or school or church that they gave up and did something interesting instead.

Papa snaps on the radio, twists knobs, punches buttons, and gets several kinds of static before he remembers the thing went dead last summer. He sighs in Lucky smoke, then sighs it out again. I wish he'd say something. Maybe he's tired of me always joking. Maybe he'd like me to be serious for a change. "What's it really like," I ask, "I mean, what do you actually *do* inside the mill?"

"Nothin' much," he mumbles.

"Do you ever do anything you *like* doing in there?"

He sucks his Lucky right down to his fingertips. "Don't matter," he says. "I'd still have to do it."

"What does Roy do?"

"'Bout the same."

"But what really goes on?" I ask. "After all these years I don't even know."

"Nothin' much," he mutters again.

I look at the mill: the night lights have all come on — whole constellations of them — spotlights and floodlights and huge square-bulbed power lights, suspended and shining from walls and wires, lighting the fog from here to the middle of the Columbia; the mill's got its own railway system, with full-sized boxcars rolling in and out of buildings; it's got its own fleet of tugs, dragging football-field-sized log rafts, one after the other, in off the river; it's got wings as big as whole office buildings, with snarls of exposed vents and flumes and overhead or underground pipes feeding them a steady river's worth of water, some of the pipes and flumes big enough to drive semis through; I can count fourteen lighthouse-sized smokestacks just from where we're sitting, with steam pouring so thick out of nine of them that they look like the source of every cloud on earth; I can feel the fog vibrating from the machinery in the building behind the giant clock. I look back at Papa. "Sure doesn't *look* like nothin' much."

He rubs his temples. "Look," he says irritably. "This mill is a bunch of machines making paper out of trees. Me and Roy and a thousand other yo-yos work the machines. That's all it is, Kincaid. You seen one mill, you seen 'em all."

"But I've never seen even one! Not on the inside."

"Then you're lucky," he says. As if that's that.

But why should it be? It's not as if him sitting there sucking down cigarettes till they stain his fingers orange is more important than talking to me. No longer trying to keep the defiance out of my voice, I ask, "How *exactly* do they make paper out of trees?"

Sliding another cigarette up out of his shirt, Papa mutters, "Where's that Roy?"

"How do they make paper out of trees?" I repeat. "I want to know."

"It's complicated," he says.

"I'm smart," I tell him.

"If you were smart," he says, "you'd know that how mills make paper out of trees isn't worth talkin' about."

"What if I own a mill someday?"

"If you were smart," he says, "you'd know you won't be owning any mills."

"If I was smart," I snap right back, "maybe I could figure out a way to get my own *dad* to talk to me now and then."

He turns on me. His eyes are slits. "You're runnin' off at the mouth and thinkin' it's clever," he says. "And I've had enough."

"You'd call *any* talking runnin' off at the mouth!" I tell him.

"*One more word*," he says, his mouth a slit now too. "You want to know about the mill, look out the goddamned window."

I look out the goddamned window. It's too goddamned foggy and dark to see. "If the place where you spend every day of your life isn't worth talkin' about," I ask, "what is?"

"*You're* the smart one," he says, and the words are literally muffled by his mouthful of smoke. "You tell me," he says, inhaling it.

I try to think of something great — something truly *fascinating* — just to show him. And to my surprise, I do. "There's a harelip at church!"

This seems to get his attention, but it's not exactly how I meant to begin. "She, uh, she's just my age. And she looks normal, and seems nice enough for a hare — er, she *is* nice. Except when she goes to talk, the lip makes everything sound like it starts with *n*. Like baseball would be *nasenall*, or Jesus *Nyeesus*."

He smokes his Lucky.

"The thing is, there's an operation that'd fix her right up, but her parents won't let her have it. They claim the lip's a cross, see. Like Christ's cross. And some people think the parents are nuts, and some think they're right. So what I wondered was, what do you think?"

"Take a vote," he sighs.

I feel myself getting mad. It makes me talk even faster. "Her name's Vera, and she's a good person, you'd like her I'll bet. Except there's one thing about her, besides the lip I mean, which isn't exactly normal, and I don't know if you'd like this thing or not."

Smoke runs like water up his nostrils. He stares straight ahead at nothing. I can tell he doesn't give a shit what the thing about Vera even is. Which makes me all the more determined to describe it.

"She likes to pray, see. And I don't mean like Irwin or even Mama like it. I mean she makes up these prayers — great big long suckers — and says 'em right in front of everybody. It's not like showing off. It's like they just *pour* out of her, like she'd die or something if she held them in. Except every time Vera opens her mouth every kid in the place starts snickerin' and snortin', and the grownups get mad, and nobody listens, and the whole place goes nuts. Yet every week, when Brother Beal asks for the closing prayer, Vera, knowing what'll happen, *still* raises her hand, *wanting* to say it!"

Papa doesn't react.

"Seems weird, doesn't it? But brave too. Don't you think?"

No answer

"She said one today, and they laughed so bad Beal started hollering '*Thank you, Vera*,' just hoping to end the noise. But it was like she couldn't hear, like the noise never mattered, because she really *was* praying, see, not just pretending, so no one counted to her, except maybe — *God*, or something."

Papa's face is so empty I shut my eyes to keep from having to see it. I want to shut my mouth too, but I feel a little like Vera must have felt; this thing has me in its grip; I've *got* to speak. "We talked about it, driving home — about Vera's parents calling the lip her cross and all. And Mama said we shouldn't take sides. She said, 'Judge not lest ye be judged.' Then Irwin said that when we see somebody with a cross we should help them carry it, like the guy did for Jesus in the Bible. But then Everett hauled off and said, 'Great, Winnie! Does it mean beat up the sixty twerps who laugh at her? Does it mean we wink and flirt with her as if the lip isn't ugly as sin and her parents aren't batty as hell for leaving it that way? Does it mean we should mangle our own lips *nand nall snart snalking nike niss*? Or is it just a piece of pious crap you're belchin' up to keep from having to do anything *real* to help her?'

"And man oh man! Mama got so mad I thought she was going to get us in a wreck…But then Peter broke in in that calm way of his that grabs your attention even better than Mama or Everett getting mad. There were some crucial things Vera's parents were forgetting about crosses, was what Peter said. One was that Jesus was nailed to His by *enemies*, not by Mary and Joseph. And another, he said, was that it killed Him. Christ's cross killed Him. We've got to remember what crosses are, Peter said. They're not just decorations

on steeples. They're murder weapons, he said, the same as guns, or gas chambers, or electric chairs. Only much, much slower. So Vera's parents, he said, were one of two things. They were either fools without the slightest idea what Christianity or crosses are. Or they were unbelievably evil.

"And not even Mama could argue with that. But then Everett spoke up again, saying that if any of us *really* wanted to help Vera, we would march straight up to her parents next Sabbath, and tell them exactly what Pete had just told us. And you should've seen Irwin! He got all excited and started nodding his head like he not only agreed but planned on doing it. But when Mama saw him in the rearview mirror, she said, '*Don't you dare!*' But I wouldn't be surprised if he *does* dare, Papa! I really think Winnie might! So what do *you* think? I mean, *should* he? Do you think Irwin should tell them?"

"Tell who what?" he murmurs, rubbing his eyes —

And suddenly something in me hurts more than I can stand. "Weren't you *listening*? Didn't you *hear*?"

He takes a drag so long and deep it can't leave his lungs by the time he needs to breathe again, so he inhales the same smoke twice. "I don't know what all goes on at your church," he says. "That's your mother's department."

I want to control myself, I want to calm down, but I also want to slug Papa so hard I knock the smoke right out of his head. Because it's a *lie*. It's a bald-faced, idiotic lie for him to sit there with his wrecked thumb and dead eyes telling me that Vera and her lip and his own sons and crosses are all "Mama's department." "Quit fidgeting," he tells me. And I can barely keep from blurting that he'd fidget too if his father was a liar. "What's *with* you today?" he grumbles. "You're squirmin' like a two-year-old."

I can't breathe, I can't see, I can't sit still.

"Get those muddy boots down off that glove box!" he snaps.

And out it comes: "Then *you* quit smoking!" I shout. "And quit *lying*! And quit sitting there like a goddamned *corpse* out of some damned — "

I see the fury come into his eyes, but I don't see the fist that smashes the left side of my face. My head snaps hard into the seat and bounces so quickly back to where it had been that for a moment I think, *Nothing happened.* Then my skull feels like it's caving

in. My mouth fills with blood. I cover my head and fall sideways. "Kade!" Papa cries, grabbing my shoulder. I shove his hand away, and crawl over against the door. "Oh, Jesus! Kade! I'm *sorry!*"

I feel a stabbing in my eye, and a roar like the mill's in my ear. I feel Papa's hands on me, hear wild apologies tangled in the roaring. The blood keeps welling, keeps pooling in my mouth, so I pull myself up to spit it all over his fucking car. But when I glance at him first, to be sure he's looking, I see he's white-faced, staring at his left hand — and the hand is trembling harder than I've ever seen anything human tremble. I swallow the blood, and turn back to the window.

"Oh God I'm sorry!" Papa moans through the roaring. "Kade, I'm *sorry!* But what *is* it with you? What do you *expect* from me?"

I don't answer, don't move or make a sound, except to swallow more blood.

"You know, millwork isn't *baseball*," he says, and his voice too is trembling. "You — Everett — Peter — do any of you understand that? It's not a game, not an art, it's not even a goddamned skill. It's just a dead thing I do for money so we can eat. I'm a millworker, Kade. And millworkers are the people who can't be who they wanted. Do you understand that?"

I don't answer. Let *him* see how it feels to pour your heart out to a statue.

"Listen!" he begs, sounding broken. "Please! I *never* should have hit you! I never will again. I'm terribly sorry, and want to show it. So tell me *please*, right now if you possibly can, what it is you want from me. Tell me what you and your brothers think I should be doing different, and if it's in my power, if it's possible at all, I *swear* I'll try to do it."

For a moment I say nothing, fearing I'll sob, or choke on blood, if I speak. But then words well right up with the blood, I'm helpless to stop them: "I *know* you hate the mill," I tell him, and tears come the instant I speak. "I *know* you love baseball, and aren't doing what you want. But at least Vera *fights*. She says her dopey prayers no matter what!" I lean against the door, gasping for air and strength to finish. "All I want is for *you* to fight, Papa. To fight to stay alive inside! No matter *what*."

For a moment it seems he's turned to stone again. Then I hear him moving toward me, till he's just inches away. I don't look or turn,

but I feel it now — not just his hand or voice but his entire body, right up against mine. And it's quaking like a cold wet dog's. Or Vera's when she prayed. *He's just like me!* I think, amazed despite the pain. *He's just a grownup boy, stuck in a body, stuck in a life. And his life isn't working. It's not working at all. And he's got no father, his mother can't understand, he's got no one to help him fix it.*

Feeling this, knowing it, I turn and try to hold my father, as he's often held me. He makes a small rasping sound when my arms slide round him, then wraps me up, very gently, and holds me back. He says nothing more, but I feel his broken breath, his broken love, his fear and heartbeat. ✎

Becoming a mother was to step through a door I imagined would be as familiar as my own past — after all, I was a child once, had observed my own mother, other mothers with children — but if I had known the transformation that awaited me, I'm not sure I'd have taken that first step.

I was shocked and depressed after my baby came, sure there was something wrong with me, that my confused, unmaternal, helpless fear was perverse, sick, bad. I remember spending a lot of time rocking myself and my baby in a borrowed, one-armed rocking chair. Did it rain every day, or was it just my imagination? Jim was away working in the furniture factory where he had recently nearly lost a finger. On a tight budget, isolated with a semi-rural case of cabin fever, no electricity, I rationed propane for hot water — and the nine-volt batteries for the radio, my big joy. I would cry when the batteries died while preparing my daughter's dinner bottle of formula.

My baby was born sickly, requiring frequent hospitalization. I didn't believe the experts when they told me it hadn't been my fault, although during pregnancy I had avoided coffee, liquor, drugs, even tea, except herbal. I'd taken my vitamins, done only low-impact aerobics. Was I being punished for my ambivalence? I hadn't been sure I really wanted a baby, unlike my girlfriends who were still single and noting the biological *tick tock* with despair. For me, pregnancy was a deeply mystical force I'd been ineffective at warding off. My other friends had children in their teens or twenties. How had they done it? Why were their kids so great, and how did they cope, and how did they get from there to here?

Dysfunctional was the term in vogue for women with feelings like mine.

Ah, the joy. The pain of joy. To be forced to love someone who would only grow up to leave me. To love and know someone who was so innocent and good and for whom I was completely responsible. The telephone became another lifeline: to doctors, to friends. Maxine, drawing on her England-during-the-Blitz experience, helped me cope with no electricity. I could keep a formula bottle cool by wrapping it in layers of newspapers. Renee talked me down, allowing me to feel scary feelings — anger, frustration, indignation. And Jane —

my only childless buddy, who stuck with me as I de-glamorized, de-single-ized, and turned into Wilma Flintstone, a.k.a. Momma Bear.

Those first four horrible months, my head began to fill with voices, as if I were a kind of mad radio program crammed full of Noam Chomsky, Oldie Goldie Platter Spinners, Rosie's traffic report, 'Morningside,' 'Union Made from Co-op,' right-wing Nashville C&W, Chicks-on-Sticks bubble gum, AM ski reports, Larry King, new wave, new jazz, new age, letters from my girlfriends, advice, recipes, home remedies, tears, hugs.

Was I drowning or was I waving?

Letters, telephone lines, and radio waves in my brain kept me afloat: *SOS. SOS. You are tuned to Momz Radio. Esta es Radio Mamasita. Ici Radio Maman, bonjour!*

My friend, Adah, asked me, "Where did that single life go?" Who was this exhausted, fat, miserable shrew who spent all her time now in playgrounds, or cooking, shopping, cleaning, wiping up poop, worrying, rocking, soothing? I was so tired, gray-haired suddenly, with time for nothing except child care, and on top of that, I was invisible. So normal, I was just a statistic. People walked right over me, my baby, the stroller, the diaper bag. Michele Landsberg wrote: "Women and children, last." Why hadn't I seen this before? What planet was I living on? Oh, right. The *single* planet. The land of time and the luxury of being alone.

Becoming a mom provided immediate entry into Feminism 403. The emotional and historical barnacles encrusting the role of mother were shocking. I was an accomplice in my own oppression at home. My experience of parenting *was* different from a man's, and I resented being punished for it. I was — and still am — looking for a part-time job where I could combine child care and working. Why was this so hard? All the magazines that talked about the revolution in the workplace — new skills, new attitudes, job-sharing, daycare on worksite — on what planet did it exist? The anthropomorphic world of children, of *Babar, Curious George, Dr. Seuss,* Ladybird picture books, Robert Munch, Beatrix Potter, "Sesame Street," and Mickey Mouse was exquisite and yet, as a society, we seemed to hate animals and children. We were exterminating whole species daily and pushing a growing number of children below the poverty line in the battle zones of abuse, war, violence, dwindling resources, and rationed love. We sentimentalized mothers, children, and animals while doing systemic violence to them.

I felt angry.

But I turned on. I wrote, performed, made art — barely — inside tiny windows of opportunity. Jan Kudelka kept three typewriters around her house so she could type a line or two of her playscript while tending both her pre-school-aged children.

Susan Swan testified, on Erika Ritter's radio show: "Single mom, writer... Yup, something had to go, and at times it did — the writing."

I wondered if I would survive, so tired and impatient, worrying whether I'd kill my child, flee my partner, escape to Morocco, the South Pacific. There was no place for an abandoning mother to go. Men walked out on their kids, unpunished. Or stayed to become domesticated — caught, caged up with women and children. How many abandoning mothers did anyone know?

It was easy to leave it all to mom, because mom picked up his socks when he was a kid but made his sister pick up her own. *Real* commitment to work and success was defined as one foot on the corporate ladder and the other in a cardiac-arrest unit. Because a baby was of mother born and suckled by her, and she was so busy, she looked like she knew what she was doing.

I didn't know what I was doing. Why was I expected to be an instant expert at motherhood skills?

By the time my daughter was a year old, I was determined to do something with the voices filling my head. I successfully applied for a Canada Council Explorations Grant to do a series of interviews, writings, lullabies — in different languages, with music — by, for, and about moms. I interviewed nine moms, solicited moms' writing from across Canada and in some parts of the U.S.A. Well-meaning Bible thumpers sent me psalms and prayers. Baby-product catalogues arrived. Eventually I got 75 responses from fabulous women who were moms: poems, journals, recipes, anecdotes, essays — handwritten, typewritten, word-processed or scribbled on napkins — some very professional, inquiring about payment and copyright, some sad and shocking, all passionate, true-life stuff. "Momz Radio" gave women permission to cut the crap about motherhood. Mostly poor women, but not all, unsentimentally shattered the mommy myths of eternal sacrifice, eternal niceness, eternally perfect nurturer, and identified mommy work as being hard, invisible, unpaid, saddling women with enormous cultural/political/spiritual expectations, double-sided

morality, judgment. The enormous changes, physically, emotionally, that motherhood brought to women of every class, creed, nationality, income, age, were shared and acknowledged publicly at last.

My daughter Aretha is now two and a half. She makes jokes and kisses my ow-ies better and is a terrific hugger and a great kisser, and we can sing and dance, play the castanets and wave pink flags, laugh and cry and love each other enormously. My daughter has won me over. Dragged me kicking and screaming through the door into motherhood.

But without the other mothers in my life who revealed themselves so unstintingly to me and who, in turn, helped me to reveal myself, I would not be as strong and accepting of my motherhood as I am today.

Lori-ann Latrèmouille, *Caesar at the Mask*, charcoal on paper, 72" x 50"

Lori-ann Latrèmouille, *Carrying for the Queen*, charcoal on paper, 44" x 30"

I

On the 25th anniversary of my father's death we gathered, my mother, brother, youngest sister and I, for a late afternoon picnic at his grave. We each planned to tell one story about Father, a personal story; it couldn't be about Father the decorated WWII fighter pilot, or Father the successful defense attorney, or Father the avid competitor at bridge and croquet.

Father was not tender with his children, and that made the assignment difficult. My other sister had backed out of the event, insisting that there weren't any positive stories, none that she could remember.

We spread a red cotton tablecloth on the grass and passed around the potato salad and sandwiches. The cemetery sits on a hillside 50 miles south of Portland, Oregon, and we watched the sun slide toward the coast range as we ate. After dishing up strawberry shortcake, Toni, the youngest, began.

After she finished her weekly Saturday morning chores, Toni said, she was permitted to ride to the farm with Father. She wandered alone among the barns, the machine shop and the fields of asparagus growing red and wild and higher than her head. Toni said her love of country life and her desire to be a farmer (we were eating strawberries which she had grown on her own four-acre commercial patch) came from those bucolic Saturdays. "I will always be grateful to Father for that," she said, and she licked a glob of whipped cream off her plastic fork. She did not add that Father, immersed in accounting and marketing schemes, often forgot to bring her home.

My brother Michael pulled a cold ale from the cooler. "The last time I ever saw him, I visited him in the hospital on my way to the Rose Cup Races," Michael said. He twisted his shirt tail around the neck of the brown bottle and slipped the metal cap into his shirt pocket. "I couldn't believe it: he'd actually read up on the race in the newspaper, and memorized the names of all the drivers. It blew my mind." Michael began chugging his ale. An unspoken question hung in the air: why had it taken Father so long to acknowledge the car races which were then the passion of his son's life?

I told the only positive story I could think of: when I was seventeen, Father gave me $1,000 and told me to start a small grocery

store for the 700 workers who lived on our asparagus farm. I was to stock, open, and operate the store for the summer and report to him in September with a revenue-and-expense statement. "He had great confidence in me," I said. Michael, no doubt remembering the grocery store fiasco, gave me a look. Father had harangued me all summer about the impracticality of trying to match Safeway prices and ridiculed my *system* for collecting on accounts. Michael's look said, No wonder you're a fiction writer.

"My turn?" Mother asked, eagerly.

It is a mysterious thing in our family, but somehow the very traits of Father's that paralyzed us kids, bloomed as virtues for Mother in the heat of her unconditional love. With us he was critical, with her intelligent; with us sarcastic, with her witty; with us indifferent, with her cool and seductive.

"Go for it, Mom," Michael said.

"I could be so mad at him I'd want to kill him," she began, and we heard her voice catch. "But he could always say something to make me laugh." I turned to see her blotting her eyes with a tissue. The loss of her husband when she was only 41 was the central tragedy of her life; she has never remarried. She stopped, too stricken to go on. Any one of us might have filled in a story.

On the occasion of her release from the hospital after totaling her beautiful wood-trimmed car, Father presented her, in public with fanfare, a wrapped gift which turned out to be a gold crash helmet on which was lettered, "Help Stamp Out Station Wagons." Though none of us children were present in the fancy restaurant, I can picture her surprise, her shriek of laughter, his cocky, Bogart smirk.

We put the remains of our picnic in the cooler and folded up the tablecloth. There are no stories of evening family meals, because Father and Mother ate tête-à-tête, after the children had been fed; there are no recollections of Father's bedtime wisdom because he never ascended to the second floor of the house where we had our rooms.

There is a special frustration when a parent dies a stranger: the relationship is frozen at the moment of his death, the riddle never to be answered. We left four heavy red roses on his grave.

II

A few months after the picnic, my husband and I were invited to dinner by some friends. Ronna Neuenschwander is a well-known Portland sculptress; her husband, Baba Wagué Diakité, whom she met

while visiting his native Mali, creates ceramic art now, too (at home in Mali, all the pottery is made by women). Wagué has a very animated and recognizable style: brightly painted animals wriggle around the surfaces of his plates and pots. He is also a great host and raconteur.

Wagué served rice with peanut sauce West African style — on the floor. While we Americans tried an assortment of uncomfortable positions, Wagué lay at his ease, stretched out like a tribal chieftain.

"In my country," Wagué said, "when we greet some person, we first ask 'How is your father?' and 'How is your mother?' If someone does not ask you these questions, it means that person does not really love you; they do not care about you."

"But you wouldn't ask a very old person," I protested.

"Oh, yes, you must always ask. My old grandmother, I ask her 'How is your father?'"

"But her father would be dead!"

"In Mali, every person has a father and a mother. If your father dies, you find a new father. Maybe it is your little grandson; maybe it is a boy you see in the village. You call him my 'little father.' When I see my grandmother, I ask about her father, and she knows I love her."

"I've gone for twenty-five years without a father: could I get a new one?"

Wagué sat up momentarily to reach a handful of fresh greens. "In my country," he said, "we would not wait so long."

III

I decided on a baby so that I'd get a father who would last. And I had a lot of babies to choose from. Ten years ago my girlfriends were still struggling to establish careers, early motherhood would have presented road blocks on the fast track. But now with their jobs guaranteed, family, many have decided, is what's missing from life.

Samuel Philip Sellers was born July 29, 1989, and from birth, he liked people. Because Sam let me hold him for long periods of time, smiling up at me with the calm, amused eyes of a little Bodhisattva, I imagined that he liked me in particular.

If I chose Sam, I would have the opportunity to "bring up father" to my expectations. This time around, I would be the empowered

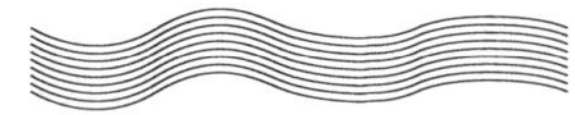

adult. How could I cultivate a loving and valuable father-daughter relationship? I made a few notes:

– tell feelings (not just anger: include thanksgiving, confusion, etc.)

– be up front about failure; welcome sympathy

– share activities – fish North Santiam? learn from library book?

Sam's parents were close friends in Seattle, where I used to live. Lucy is a documentary filmmaker and Don has traveled around the world, shooting and editing documentaries for the PBS series "Frontline." They met in the Stanford film program, were married in 1986, and Sam is their first child.

I was sitting in the sunlit kitchen of Don and Lucy's home on Queen Anne Hill when I told Wagué's story.

"I want a new father and I'd like it to be Sam."

Don, who has renounced travel since the birth of Sam, was perched on a kitchen stool, drinking espresso from a small blue cup. "The lucky little son of a gun," he said.

Lucy was standing at the sink with her back to me, holding a glass of water under the tap, with baby Sam balanced on her left hip. She turned and smiled. "So how do you do it? Just pick him out and that's it?"

"Basically," I said.

Sam celebrated his first Father's Day six weeks before his first birthday.

IV

Kinship weaves the tribe together. In Wagué's village, it weaves so tight a fabric that even the gods could not unravel it. Wagué was named for his maternal grandfather: Baba means father; Wagué was the name bestowed upon his grandfather by the villagers, an honorific which means "good man." Wagué was given these names by his mother, who chose Wagué to replace her own father when he died.

When Wagué married, his wife became his mother's "little mother." Now Wagué's mother looks forward to the arrival of Wagué's child so that she can have a new "little brother or sister."

People feel a great hunger for community, but in contemporary society they can't satisfy this hunger within their families, which tend to be fractured and isolated. Instead, they look outside to friends, business colleagues, neighbors at the sub-division, apartment building or houseboat moorage.

My new family has been a shortcut to community. My relationship with Sam's parents has changed, quickened. After I moved 180 miles away, our friendship might have become a once-a-year dinner, and then dwindled to Christmas cards, and then to memories. But now that their infant son has a daughter living in Portland, we are obliged to stay in close touch by phone, letters and frequent visits. This obligation is a happy one. I cannot doubt my welcome in Sam's home: I am family.

Every two months, Sam's parents send me an updated photograph which I put up on our refrigerator. Visitors to our kitchen spot Sam within the first minute. "Who is this incredible baby?" they ask.

I remember the day my brother Michael first saw Sam's picture. He had come to dinner and brought some Brie and started to open the refrigerator. "Why do I seem to know this baby?" he said, staring at Sam.

"That's my new father," I said, stirring pasta at the stove.

Michael stashed the cheese and walked over to the stove, where steam fogged his eyeglasses. He put his arm around my shoulder. "Do you want to explain that?" he asked.

Now my "real" family is eager to meet Sam — their "little father"? Michael's daughter's "little grandfather"? Mother's new "little husband"?

V

So many women feel unloved by their fathers, as the bank accounts of therapists attest.

Because of my relationship with Sam, I now see my father — my first father, Parker Gies — through bifocals. Through one lens he's tough and distant. But through the other lens, he's just like Sam — a handsome, hopeful boy child, wanting love and eager to give it. In a photograph taken when Father was five, he is dressed in a white shirt and short pants and gazes out with the same trusting half-smile I've seen on Sam. How did my own father, blessed like Sam with health and responsible parents, turn out to be so cold? Was it the expectation that men be tough and unfeeling? Was it the War, where he saw one buddy blown up directly in front of him on the runway at Clark Field, and the other go mad with fear and anxiety? Was it the all-consuming preoccupation with making money? Whose idea was it that listening, holding, and caring were Mother's department? Why was providing orthodontia and a college education the sum of his involvement?

When I ask these questions, I see he was cheated, too.

With Sam it will be different; he is already a successful father.

Years from now, I imagine, Sam may spend a summer evening at my grave. Maybe his own daughter (my "little sister") will be with him. Since I don't plan to die for awhile, let's say she's fourteen. They've finished the potato salad when she says, "Dad, I think I got a C on my French test."

Sam puts his arm around her and asks, "How does that make you feel?"

"I don't know if I like French," she says.

"Try not to tense up about it," he says. "You can take something else next year; just don't make an enemy of it." He feels her shoulders relax as she sighs deeply and leans into his windbreaker.

"I think you're a real good dad."

"I was lucky," Sam says. "I learned to be a father when I was a little kid."

The girl knows he's talking about me, of course. Sliding out from under his arm, she dishes up strawberry shortcake. "How do you think she learned it, Daddy?"

"She had a father of her own, before me. He died when she was young," Sam says.

"She learned it from him?"

"She did," Sam agrees. "But she learned it the hard way."

They sit silently, eating their dessert, as metallic streaks of rose and orange kindle the western sky. ⌇

LEAVING HOME

William Stafford

What you leave is the front porch in the evening,
dove sounds, the way you felt leaning back
in the squeaking swing, how your mother
pushed her hair back while ironing.

This isn't anyone's intention — you didn't decide
to be dutiful and remember your home. It's like a big
hook that reaches for you and you're caught in your
    breath.
But you just go on and no one can tell how you feel.

Somebody says, "Did you like your family? Were you
happy at home?" Now it's your turn to keep
anyone from knowing how those days were the
    whole world,
and that now it's ended. You look away and say yes.

I haven't told this before. By our house on the plains before
I was born my father planted a maple. At night after bedtime
when others were asleep I would go out and stand beside it
and know all the way north and all the way south. Air from the
fields wandered in. Stars waited with me. All of us ached with
a silence, needing the next thing, but quiet. We leaned into
midnight and then leaned back. On the rise to the west the radio
tower blinked — so many messages pouring by.

A great surge came rushing from everywhere and wrapped all
the land and sky. Where were we going? How soon would our house
break loose and become a little speck lost in the vast night? My
father and mother would die. The maple tree would stand right
there. With my hand on that smooth bark we would watch it all.
Then my feet would come loose from Earth and rise by the power of
longing. I wouldn't let the others know about this, but I would
be every where, as I am right now, a thin tone like the wind, a
sip of blue light — no source, no end, no horizon.

The word kept turning over in his head, like a dime in his pocket, or a lucky charm on a key chain.

It was a word he had read in a *National Geographic* magazine, a Mayan word, and it buoyed him up and carried him along as he rode the bus downtown through the gray morning.

"Hachuch," said the bus doors as they opened. "Hachuch," they said as they closed again. Samuel walked the last five blocks to the Arthur Hubble Bible College, where he took classes in accounting and theology.

Hachuch, thought Samuel as he sat at a desk too small for him and studied the Gospel of John. The word fascinated him, although it didn't apply to anything in his life. It was almost like a Hebrew word, like an ancient name from the Old Testament, but it wasn't.

One day Samuel walked into a grocery store to buy an apple for his lunch. It was about two blocks from the college, and he had walked down Fifth Street for a respite from the brown rooms and black chalkboards of Hubble's. He handed the apple to the girl at the cash register, and the word leaped into his mind. She was short, with black, shoulder-length hair, and a nose which continued the curve of her forehead. She had wide, heavy-lidded eyes, and a fleeting, wide smile when she handed him his change. The word described her exactly, for *hachuch* is a Mayan word for pretty, and she was dark and vivid in the gray neutralness of Los Angeles in February.

Samuel was in heaven. Almost every day, he stopped in the little store to buy an apple, an orange, or a candy bar. Sometimes the girl, Gloria, was there, and sometimes an older woman who might have been related.

Samuel's parents, with whom he lived, began to wonder about him, and his father, an Evangelical minister, commented on the extravagance of buying lunch every day instead of taking it with him. Samuel said nothing, but continued with his classes and with his part-time bookkeeping job at Kresge's Five and Dime. He always turned his paycheck over to his father, and a few dollars were counted out to him for bus fare and *cual quier cosa* — this and that, which included his fruit-buying spree.

Samuel was twenty-four, and the second oldest of six children. His

parents expected all of their children to serve the church in some capacity, the boys as ministers, the girls, God willing, as ministers' wives. It was 1952.

One Saturday, when Samuel couldn't stand it and took the bus downtown to the grocery store, one of his little brothers followed him.

"A girlfriend!" he yelled, when Samuel came outside. "You have a girlfriend."

Samuel denied this, but at supper was questioned by his parents. He admitted that he liked Gloria, but that he had never really had a conversation with her. He only knew her name because someone else had come in and talked to her while Samuel was in the store.

His parents didn't know what to do.

"We don't know anything about her," said the Reverend Armadio later that evening to his wife, "and his preoccupation with her is interfering with his studies."

"But he is twenty-four," his wife reminded him. "He's almost old enough to get married. Matteo was twenty-five." The eldest, Matteo, lived in Pasadena with his wife.

The Reverend Armadio went to bed troubled that night.

"You must invite her over for supper," the Reverend told Samuel the next morning. "We have a right to know who you are interested in."

Samuel didn't know what to do. He had always been very shy, and the quick, undemanding smiles with which Gloria had treated him had been the only reason he'd been bold enough to return.

"You look like you study too hard," she had said once, pointing at his books on the counter.

"Oh, no," he had stammered. "I like to study." And he had grabbed his books and fled.

Two weeks went by, and nothing more was heard of Gloria in the Armadio household. Samuel had been too mortified by his father's ultimatum to return to the store.

"Well, I guess he wasn't so interested in her after all," said the Reverend to his wife, trying not to look too satisfied. "He shouldn't marry until he's finished school and is at least an assistant pastor, anyway."

"You did," said his wife.

"That was different," he answered. "I was more mature than he is."

But Samuel couldn't stop thinking about Gloria. Now the two words, *hachuch* and Gloria, rolled like jingling coins in his head. The words and numbers on the blackboards wouldn't hold still before his eyes, and old Mr. Jenkins began to frown at the gaunt youth with the faraway look, and mutter about "secular thoughts."

Finally, Samuel could stand it no longer. He returned to the store, introduced himself, and asked Gloria if she would have supper with his family.

"Well," she said, surprised, and looked around at the vegetables and candy and magazines as though gathering her feelings.

"Just a minute. Let me ask my mother."

She disappeared behind the patterned green cloth that curtained off the back of the store. In a minute, Gloria returned with the older woman he had seen before. She surveyed Samuel with a slow, dignified look.

"What is your name?" she asked.

"Samuel Armadio, *a su servicio*."

"And what do you do?"

"I go to college at Hubble Bible College, down the street, and I work part-time at Kresge's."

"Hmm," she said, and nothing more. Samuel began to feel very warm, and ran his hand through his short, curly hair.

"He lives with his family," said Gloria. "His father is a minister."

Her mother still didn't say anything, but continued to look at Samuel, who was beginning to have difficulty breathing.

"Well," she said, finally, "What is your address? And your phone number?" Samuel told her, as she deliberately spelled them out on the back of an advertising flyer with a stubby pencil kept by the cash register.

"*Bueno*," she said to Gloria. "You can go."

She almost smiled at Samuel, then turned and left the shop. Gloria smiled shyly.

"Okay," she said, "what night?"

"Uh, tomorrow?"

"Okay."

So Samuel picked her up the next day in his father's black Chrysler at 5:30. Her family lived on the block behind the grocery store, a little neighborhood of colorful stucco houses which Samuel had never noticed before. Gloria's house was turquoise with lace curtains, and had a banana tree in the front yard. Younger brothers and sisters

played beneath it.

"Bye bye," they all waved.

Gloria waved back from the big, dark car. Her mother watched from the window.

Gloria wore a navy blue suit and big, white beads that shone like her teeth and eyes. Samuel could hardly believe this was happening to him.

Besides his parents and brothers and sisters, Samuel's two unmarried aunts came to dinner to see who this Gloria was. The dining room was very crowded. After his father prayed, his mother served pot roast, Spanish rice, and overdone vegetables, and his brothers and sisters beamed at Gloria, watching her every move.

"So," began his aunt Arcelia, soon into the dinner, "you work in a grocery store?"

"Yes," said Gloria. "It is my parents'."

"And you're out of school?"

"Yes," she said, "I graduated last year."

The questions went on and on, but Gloria answered each of them with grace and patience, until even the Reverend Armadio couldn't help but smile.

Afterwards, Samuel drove her home, while the family assessed her.

"She's nice!" said the children. "Maybe her father will let us have candy."

"Shhh!" said Mrs. Armadio. "You don't need any candy."

"*Morena*," said the aunts to each other. "She's too dark. Their children would be black like Indians." And they patted their own carefully powdered cheeks.

The Reverend Armadio didn't say much of anything. "We'll see," he said, "what happens."

After that, Samuel went to see Gloria whenever he could. He took gum for her brothers and sisters, and as the weather warmed up, he and Gloria took long walks.

Gloria described Samuel's family to her mother. She told how he did whatever he was told, even when he didn't agree, and about the aunts who seemed to have a say in everything that happened.

"You must be careful," said her mother, "that you don't end up marrying the family, instead of his marrying you."

So Gloria decided on a plan. One day she said, "I wish you wouldn't wear a hat."

"Why not?" asked Samuel, her hand tucked into the crook of his elbow as they walked.

"I don't like it," she answered.

"I'll get a different one."

"No," she said, "I don't like hats on you at all."

So Samuel stopped wearing a hat. His mother noticed immediately.

"Where's your hat?"

"I'm not taking it."

"Why not?"

"I don't want to."

"You'll catch a cold."

"It's April, Mama. I don't need it."

"You should always wear a hat when you go out. People will think we have no breeding."

Samuel said nothing at all, and slipped out the door.

His mother guessed that it must have something to do with Gloria, and began to watch him more closely.

"That girl is putting ideas into his head," she told Reverend Armadio. "He doesn't want to obey his own mother."

"Why can't you date girls from the church?" the Reverend asked Samuel that evening. "Gloria's probably not even Christian."

"She comes to church with me," he replied. "Besides, all the girls at church are my cousins."

"They are not!" said the Reverend.

"Yes they are!" squeaked Samuel's little sister Lucila, "except Rosa," then dissolved into a fit of giggling.

Rosa was very fat, and was always paying attention to Samuel. Samuel blushed deeply, and no one dared say anything else.

"You know," said Gloria about three weeks later, "I wish you would bring me flowers sometimes."

So every Saturday afternoon after that, Samuel brought her a beautiful bouquet of flowers he bought from the Chinese florist. It cost him seventy-five cents, and took all of his lunch money, so that he got thinner than ever.

"Look how skinny he is," said his aunts, talking behind their hymnals in church. "She's cast a spell over him, given him the eye, and he's wasting away."

They put on their gloves and adjusted their hats before going out into the hot sun. Gloria just smiled, and always said hello to each of

them, so that they couldn't help but admit that she had good manners.

Samuel finished his coursework for the year, and went to work for Kresge's full time in the summer. He had received all A's in his accounting classes, and one B in a Bible class.

"You're not paying attention in school," said his father. "If you have to date, why don't you meet a nice girl at the Bible college?"

"They're all *Americanas*," he replied. "And they don't date Mexican boys. The school doesn't allow it." The Reverend Armadio didn't say anything else. He had considered the founder, Arthur Hubble, a former missionary to Mexico, a friend until his death five years earlier.

For the first time, Samuel was beginning to understand why his brother Matteo hardly came to visit anymore.

The hot summer wore on, and Samuel worked Monday through Friday at Kresge's, and half a day on Saturday. On Saturday afternoons, he and Gloria would walk downtown and look at the shops. Samuel had never really looked at store windows before. In them were things too wonderful to even imagine owning, from colorful lawn furniture to clothes. Chalk-white mannequins demonstrated the use of barbecues and lawnmowers, and wore "resort clothing". He liked to look in the bookstore, and even bought a used book now and then. His father didn't object to books, as long as they weren't too worldly.

"Look at that hat," Gloria said on one of their strolls. "Isn't it pretty?"

On impulse, Samuel took her inside to try it on. It was a much nicer store than any he had ever been in before.

Gloria asked the clerk, a middle-aged woman with painted eyebrows, to see the hat. The woman excused herself and went to talk to a woman at the cash register. She came back and said, "I'm sorry, that one is for display purposes only. We're sorry we can't help you."

Gloria looked at the woman, started to say something, and thought better of it. She smiled and they left.

Samuel was confused. "Why couldn't you try on the hat?"

Gloria looked at him as though for the first time that day.

"It must be a store where they don't serve Mexicans."

Samuel felt a rush of anger and gripped Gloria's elbow tightly as they walked. He did not mind if people treated him that way, after all they might mistake him for a *pachuco* (except that he no longer

wore a hat), but it galled him that Gloria could be refused service in a store.

"Maybe it's because you were with me," he said.

"No," said Gloria, then started to laugh. "No, it's not because I'm with you." She held up her dark arm against his brownish yellow one. They both started to laugh.

Samuel couldn't get the hat incident out of his head. He went to work and came home, and lay awake at night thinking about things. For the first time, he realized that his parents probably avoided certain stores and restaurants for reasons other than the prices.

"Look at him," said his mother as he walked quickly out of the house one day, head bowed in thought "He is obsessed."

Two weeks later, Samuel took Gloria back by the store. A girl was in the window changing the display. Without warning, Samuel swung Gloria, wide-eyed, through the doorway.

"We'd like to see that hat, please," he said a little too loudly.

"Of course," said the girl standing in the window display.

"I was just about to take it down. We're about to get our fall line in." The other sales clerk was nowhere to be seen.

Gloria tried the hat on before a full length mirror. It was a white straw hat with a large brim, and had a little bunch of red cherries on one side. With her pearly white teeth and her white beads, Samuel thought she looked like a princess.

"We'll take it," said Samuel in a voice which Gloria had never heard before. She hugged him right there in the store.

When Samuel went home with only part of his pay, his parents were very angry.

"You have no sense of responsibility," said his father, and shut the door to his study.

"Go!" said his mother. "You have already made your choice," and she put her hands to her chest as though her heart were breaking. "You might as well marry her, since we mean so little to you now."

And so, at the end of that summer, he did. Everyone at the church came to the wedding, and the Reverend Armadio officiated. Gloria's mother looked proud and satisfied in the navy blue suit Samuel had first seen on Gloria. All the old women commented on how dark Gloria looked in white, and all the men thought how pretty she was.

Hachuch, thought Samuel as she came down the aisle. Gloria looked right at him and smiled her serene smile, the white straw hat on her head.

Samuel went to work as an accountant for Kresge's Los Angeles headquarters, and didn't finish Bible school. As a result, the hopes of the family were pinned on the next oldest boy, Julio, who was twelve years old.

Samuel and Gloria rented a house on a steep hillside in Echo Park, where they grew flowers and herbs in the yard. When Gloria wrapped her brown arms and generous legs around Samuel at night, he didn't think anything at all.

Some of their children were black like Indians, and some of them were not. ❦

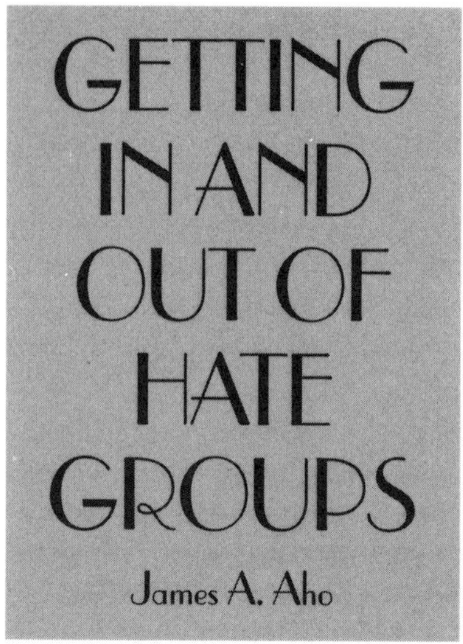

Popular legend holds racism and bigotry to be products of the old confederate states. While this is not entirely without justification, it has become decreasingly accurate since the early 1970s. The best data available demonstrates that the highest concentration of right-wing groups is found in the Rocky Mountain and Pacific Coast states. These have rates at least two times those of the Deep South. Of these states, Montana, Idaho, and Oregon are the three top-ranked extremist locales in the country, with Wyoming, Colorado, Arizona, Washington, and Alaska filling in the top ten. Montana alone boasts nearly 20 right-wing headquarters per 500,000 residents, Idaho 17.

Being associated with a university in Idaho, a day's drive from the town provisionally named as capital of a five state Pacific Northwest racially-pure Aryan "homeland," I have been favorably situated to research the extremist movement "up close and personal," as it is said. This research program was inaugurated in January 1985, about a month after a shoot-out on Whidbey Island, Puget Sound, Washington, between several hundred Federal agents and members of a terrorist group calling itself the *Bruders Schweigen* (Secret Brotherhood).

The subtitle of the book growing out of my research — *Idaho's Christian Patriots* — has stirred some controversy, critics maintaining that my subjects are neither patriots nor, above all, Christians; they are neo-Nazis. This criticism can be deflected easily. First, as almost everyone knows, abstract biblical passages are and have been subject for centuries to multiple interpretation, justifying everything from sexual asceticism to orgies (as in the case of the notorious Children of God), from pacifism to the blood-thirsty violence of the Crusades. Second, Judeophobia, far from having nothing to do with Christianity has been, again for centuries, to use Rosemary Ruether's phrase, "the left-hand of Christianity." A substantial statistical association between Christian fundamentalism and anti-Semitism persists in America to this day. What this all means is that people with a

fondness for Adolf Hitler have a rich treasury of church decretals, homilies, and pastoral literature upon which to draw. Rev. Richard Butler, pastor of the Aryan Nations Church in Idaho, has placed his two favorite volumes near the phone at his desk: *Mein Kampf* and the *King James Bible*. Not only does he fail to see any irony in this juxtaposition, he maintains that Jesus Christ was an Aryan and racist like himself.

One of the goals of my research was to explain causally why some people join hate groups. Or to say it more candidly, what is it that distinguishes "those people" from the rest of us. Needless to say, what happens to many naive researchers happened to me as well: I was reluctantly compelled by reality first to change the tone and then the direction of my stated goal. The subsequent alterations took two forms.

First of all, I went into the field assuming that hate group affiliates would have different personal and psychological attributes than ourselves. I discovered this to be untrue. Becoming a hate group member evidently has little to do with low levels of formal education, insanity, nor alienation from conventional society. Right-wing extremists are not distinctively more transient than their more conventional peers, significantly younger, nor politically more apathetic; they are not more inclined than typical Americans to labor in what have been called "structurally isolated" occupations such as farming, logging, or mining; their marriage stability rate is comparable to, if not greater than, that of their neighbors; and the vast majority of those who have had a religious upbringing, were raised in this country's main-line denominations (although at present many belong to exclusive fundamentalist sects like the Yahweh Believers, the Gospel of Christ Ministry, the New Covenant Theocracy, the Church of the Creator, etc. The latter was founded by self-proclaimed "Pontifex Maximus" Ben Klassen, author of the *White Man's Bible*, "a powerful religious creed and program for the survival, expansion and advancement of the White Race." It has two "parishes" in Montana, one in Missoula, the other in Superior).

Second, I began my research assuming that one who joins a hate group naturally continues his affiliation. I believed that the typical career trajectory of a "neo-Nazi" was toward increasing radicalism, culminating in violence, imprisonment, and in the most extreme cases, death. As I proceeded, however, I came across a handful of individuals who had voluntarily disengaged themselves from the

Klan, the White Student Union (a racist skinhead group), or from the Christian Patriots Defense League. Furthermore, I found that these disaffections from hate, like affiliation to it, appeared to have little to do with ideological appeals. None of the informants whose stories I recorded mentioned Holocaust films, classroom instruction on the Civil Rights movement, documentation of the horrors of slavery, or any other pedagogical device as impelling them out of hate.

In short, I was confronted with a series of anomalies, and I found that the only way to accommodate them was with a variation of what sociologists call network theory. Its basic assumption: People act as they do, not so much because of their personal peculiarities (at least not these alone), but because of how they are positioned in institutional networks. As applied to the issue at hand, people join hate groups — and later disengage when they do — not because of their psychological attributes, but because of who (largely by chance) their school chums, apartment mates, co-workers, church congregants, fellow union members, neighbors, lovers, and especially family members happen to be. Of the 228 individuals on whom I was able to garner information on this question, nearly three-quarters indicated a primary group influence as the major reason for joining a hate group; about 20 percent mentioned a secondary group influence; and only 10 percent, an advertisement or a media message.

To illustrate network theory I present two case studies, the first taken from the book and illustrating the recruitment of an entire family to hate; the second from an article I later composed which depicts the reverse, migration out of hate.

Ed and Lisa Minor are the fictitious names of two congregants of the Aryan Nations Church. Lisa was raised liberal Catholic in a northern Idaho town named for the river which meanders through it. By the time she was a teen-ager her mother had long since resigned herself to a life of tedium and helplessness, providing little encouragement and even less guidance for Lisa and her sisters. Each as a result has tried to forge destinies in the world independent of the family. For her part, at 18 Lisa traveled to Moscow, Idaho to study physical therapy at the state's land grant university. This was during the late 1960s, and she became deeply involved in the local drug scene, dropping out of college and returning home a hippy. While living with her parents she went through a series of dead-end relationships with small-time drug pushers, the last of whom was a charismatic Charles Manson cult leader type. Realizing that if she did not pull

herself together and soon, hers would be a short, senseless, brutal life, Lisa turned to prayer. How this solution came to her is unclear. What is known is that she was "born again," joined a local Bible Church, and found employment as a clerk in its Christian bookstore. It was there that she met Ed.

Ed Minor's cause had for some years been the Aryan Nations Church. Raised nominally "Christian," he had already turned agnostic seeker when he learned of the church through friends at Lockheed Aircraft in Lancaster, California, where he worked as an electrical engineer. Included among these friends was Richard Butler, mentioned above as the present pastor of the church. We do not know if Butler himself recruited Ed into what was at that time Wesley Swift's congregation, but when after Swift's death Butler got control of its mailing lists and Swift's taped sermons, and moved the church's headquarters to northern Idaho in the early 1970s, Ed dropped everything to accompany him. He subsequently settled in a log cabin in the woods surrounding a nearby lake, and when the new chapel was constructed at Hayden Lake he volunteered to install the utilities.

Ed is about 20 years older than Lisa, well educated, sure of himself and of his beliefs. He was the kind of man, a stable Christian man, that Lisa had been looking for when, as was his custom, he made one of his recruitment visits to the bookstore. Lisa now lives in his shadow, bearing his children, rarely seeing visitors. She is the prototypical hippy earth mother turned barefoot, silent, pregnant wife.

Lisa and Ed were married in the newly-built Aryan Nations chapel, Rev. Butler officiating. After 13 years of marriage they boast seven children, the oldest already a teen. The children rarely attend public school, for it teaches the satanic pedagogy of "secular humanism." Nor do they attend private church school. The Aryan Nations Academy at which the "4 Rs" were taught — reading, 'riting, 'rithmetic, and race — was closed many years ago; matriculation at other church schools would be prohibitively expensive given Ed's perennial unemployment and the family's impoverishment. Nor are the children taught much at home. According to outside observers, in other words, the children are functionally illiterate. All, nonetheless, can expostulate on who is at fault for the world's ills: the Jews. Like mom and dad, all are devoted and voluble racists. What was once the faith of a single, forceful, clear-sighted personality, Ed's, has been incorporated by his wife and successfully transmitted to the next generation.

Had Lisa not been "reborn," had she not joined a Bible church and sought employment in its bookstore, Ed might never have met her, and Lisa's life would have taken some other, probably radically different trajectory. Had Ed not been an active seeker with an unrefined "Christian" outlook working by chance with Richard Butler, he likely would never have learned of the Aryan Nations Church. The seven children, on the other hand, have been born into a setting in which it is taken for granted that they are "God's battle axe and weapons of war." Unless they rebel against the hold their parents, and through them the church, have over them, they are fated to walk in their parents' footsteps. But even this is not certain. At the time of my research the eldest son was riding his bike to town every morning to play video games and "hang around." It is possible that these daily excursions will introduce him to a different social network and to a style of life opposed to Lisa's and Ed's.

Consider in this regard the case of Greg Withrow. At the July 1986 Aryan World Congress in Idaho, I quoted Withrow demanding in his keynote address that non-Aryan men, women, and children "be expelled" from America or "terminated." The utter seriousness of his demeanor, the strident anger in his voice, the "Hail victory" answering each of his exhortations, led me to believe that here is a truly dangerous man, one best placed under hourly police surveillance.

Before the year was over Withrow had publicly renounced his words, stepped down from his leadership of the White Student Union, and had declared himself converted through "love" to acceptance of his enemies. "I've said a lot of terrible things and I've spread a lot of harm; I don't want to hate anymore. I don't want to hurt anymore," he told reporters. What we have here is either an incredible effort at dissimulation or one of the most noteworthy spiritual transformations in recent record.

Withrow was raised in an emotionally cold family by a father who drank heavily. Following the inevitable divorce Withrow became in his words a "stray," living in the streets, eating out of garbage cans, sleeping in brush near libraries, and suffering the torments of prowling black teens. Winter days found him in reading rooms in the company of Mussolini, Nietzsche, and Hitler. By the age of 13 Withrow was a self-acknowledged racist with delusions of grandeur and fantasies of racist revenge. He set about translating his dreams into action. Starting at American River Junior College in Sacramento, by

the early 1980s he had founded chapters of the WSU on 30 California campuses. "We had science fiction, cartoons, skinhead rock n' roll tapes, slam dancing, t-shirts — all programmed for your mind, all oriented toward violent behavior."

In the Fall of 1986 two events shook Withrow's world. First his father died of cancer and of symptoms related to alcoholism. Withrow relates that his father "had a plan for me to be like Hitler." It was his father who had introduced him to the Klan and later to the White Aryan Resistance, then headed by his close friend Tom Metzger. (The reader may recall that in October 1990 Metzger was found liable for $12.5 million in civil damages to a black Portland, Oregon family, one of whose members was brutally slain by three skinheads acting as Metzger's agents. Metzger was not criminally implicated in the case). "I honored my father," says Withrow. "When he died it hurt. But there was also a sense of relief...I had this thought that, 'gee, maybe I don't have to carry this on anymore.'"

This may be considered the initial "push" out of racism for Withrow. The "pull" would come that November when Withrow chanced upon a cocktail waitress at the gambling club he frequented. "Sylvia" had already read about Withrow's activities in the news; evidently she refused to believe that underneath the bluff and swagger he was not a "nice guy." Following their first date, viewing the sado-masochistic movie romance *9 ½ Weeks*, Sylvia turned to Withrow and uttered the words that "just blew my mind": "I love you." Within a month Sylvia had moved into Withrow's apartment. "For the first time in my life I was just having fun...For the first time in my life, I loved someone."

Possibly sensing weakness in his composure, Withrow's followers began testing his authority. By Spring 1987 he was replaced as head of the WSU by Metzger's son. Withrow responded by publicly announcing his intention to resign from the group altogether and ridiculing its pretensions. It was then that the assaults began. In one incident three bat-wielding gang members threatened to kill him if he spoke out again. To lend credibility to their threat they broke his nose and jaw.

Withrow has since split-up with the woman who led him from the labyrinth of racial hate and has made two half-hearted attempts to poison himself. It is not easy to leave behind everything one once proclaimed to begin a new life. Nevertheless, Withrow insists that his conversion is final. "Some people might regret what's happened

to me, but they should rejoice at what's happened to my soul...I know one thing — if I live, I'm going to find peace."

Greg Withrow now works with the Anti-Defamation League of B'nai B'rith helping others like himself negotiate their way out of hate.

Hate groups with a Christian guise have long been a feature of American life. What we observe today in the Pacific Northwest is simply another outbreak of a chronic disease. Sociologists and journalists have studied this pathology for years, prescribing remedies consistent with their theories. The problem is that almost all their research has been conducted from a distance too great to afford accurate observation. As a result, stereotypes about right-wing extremism and extremists have proliferated in social science literature and popular imagination, reflecting liberal biases. Right-wingers, it is said, are characteristically poorly educated; they are socially anomic, authoritarian, status insecure, and exhibit signs of psychosis as testified to by their conspiratorial mind-set, etc. Given these alleged characteristics then it is inconceivable, goes the argument, that they could be anything other than what they are essentially.

My own field work on these same people explodes these myths. Psychologically, right-wingers are within the boundaries of clinical normalcy. Even the murderers among them, while statistically abnormal, are not certifiably insane. Sociologically, they appear to have been recruited into hate groups in a manner largely indistinguishable from how others of us have become committed to our own favorite causes, whether these are vegetarianism, scientology, environmentalism, or peace. One implication of this is that just like ourselves and our own hobbies, doctrines, and interests, those presently in the hate movement are not permanently locked into it.

We all have our fascinations and dislikes. And like others, we detest most those about whom we know the least. This renders them incapable of edifying us ethically, that is, of shocking us into the realization that "but for the grace of God there goest I." One group that many of us remain largely ignorant and fearful of and deeply hostile to is the extreme right-wing. While this is understandable given the distastefulness of its doctrine, it is no excuse for remaining ignorant. We must get out of the comforting security of our library carrels and offices, away from the colleagues who reinforce our prejudices, and into the field with our enemies. &

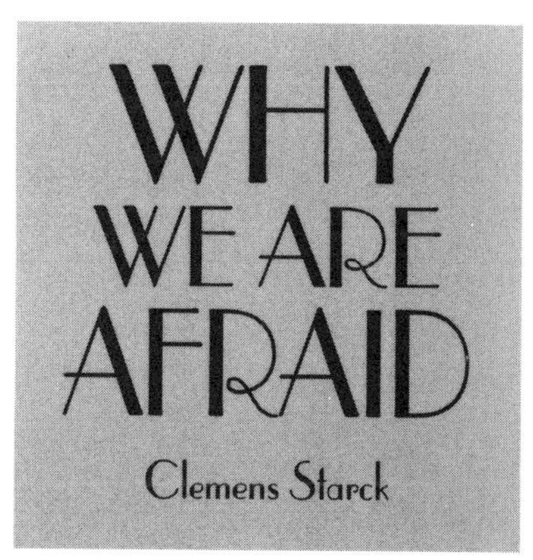

My family is bored. We have everything.
There's nothing left for us to have, except maybe
a space shuttle
or an automatic ice-cube maker.
Verily, merchandise breeds merchandise.
Every day new catalogues arrive.
But it's no use. Whatever they're selling
we've already got.

My country, too, is bored. Even more so, because
it has the space shuttle
and it can make ice cubes at a prodigious rate.
And that is why we're so afraid,
and why we need
bombers that can fly through the eye of a needle,
bullets that travel backwards and forwards,
crossbows
and harquebuses
to protect us from our enemies.

What I say, is: Enemies, when you arrive
you can have it all! I'll leave
instructions for the microwave
next to the sink in the bottom drawer.

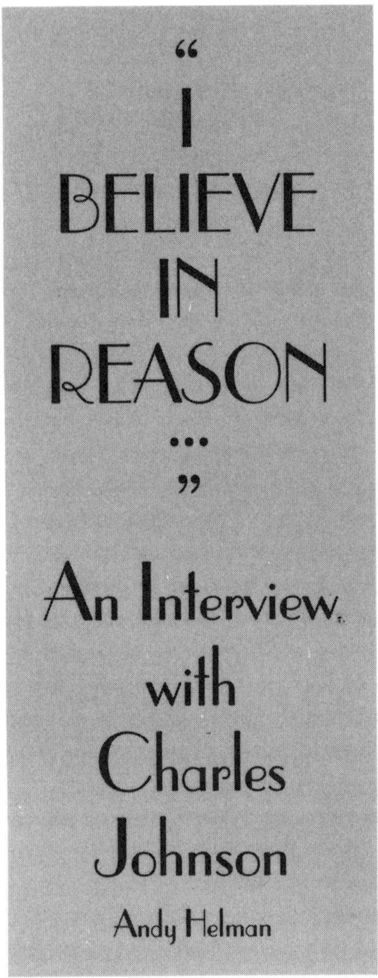

Charles Johnson, teacher, novelist, cartoonist, screenwriter, essayist, philosopher, and Buddhist, has more facets than the Hope Diamond. Hope for all people fills Johnson's heart and runs through his work with the same quiet persistence he gave to Middle Passage, *which took 18 years to complete. It was the 1990 National Book Award winner for fiction, and Johnson was the second African-American male to win the National Book Award in 37 years.*

"I believe in myself," Johnson told me in the book-filled, postage stamp of an office he's occupied since 1976 at the University of Washington. "I believe, also, in other people, and the capacity of Black people...you see what human capabilities are and that cuts across races as well...people who have it very difficult and manage to do remarkable things."

Johnson began his career at 17 as a cartoonist. He graduated from Southern Illinois University in journalism, received an M.A. in philosophy, and did graduate work in phenomenology and black literary aesthetics. His work today, he says, is black philosophical fiction, fusing Western and Eastern philosophy to better explain the black experience. Johnson has taught at the University of Washington since 1976 and was recently named to its first endowed professorship in creative writing. Among his works are Being & Race, Black Writing Since 1970; Faith and the Good Thing; Oxherding Tale *and* The Sorcerer's Apprentice.

Johnson is a low-keyed, friendly man with an easy laugh who listens as intently as he deserves to be listened to.

Andy Helman: We're living in a very volatile time. What do you see happening in a cultural sense?

Charles Johnson: This is a curious time for American culture. I think we're working our way through fundamental questions: what does it mean to be a family?, what does it mean to be an American?, and who are all the Americans?

Some people describe what we have, not as a melting pot, but rather as a salad, together but unmixed, just laying there side by side.

In terms of race relations, I think things are infinitely better than they were 30 years ago. My dad grew up in the '30s in the South; in the '60s there was no question in his mind that things were better, that there were greater opportunities for black people. And I think it's going to get better. But I think we're going to go through a period where a lot of individuals are bruised before we somehow come out on the other side.

We've entered into another dimension in the post-black power period in the late last hour of the 20th century, a dimension where people are extremely suspicious of each other — blacks and whites, people of Asian background as well as Hispanics and people who are classified as black but who are not black Americans, such as Ethiopians. There is a lot of tension and strained relations; it is very unusual to see that because I don't think it was like that to such a degree in the '60s, when I was 18, 19, 20 years old.

I think the younger kids, for example, don't have the historical context to know *how* we got here as a people, and they don't understand the civil rights movement and what that was about. And basically they sit across the room and they see other people whose skin color is different, people with whom they are competing for a shrinking number of jobs, for a shrinking number of shots at the American dream. I think the tension and strain are exacerbated by a bad economic situation. People are very worried, as they were not in the '60s, about whether they will even *get* a job, whether they will be able to afford a home. They look over there and they wonder if this group or that group is privileged because of something called affirmative action. That wonder generates a lot of tension.

I don't believe in separatism; I really don't think that's a good idea. I think it's a silly idea. We live in a very interconnected human world. Kwame Appiah, an African philosopher at Harvard, said in his most recent book, *In My Father's House,* "We are all already contaminated by each other." I think he's right; our lives are interblended. How-

ever, it seems to me there is no question that for everything we talked about in the Civil Rights Movement to make sense, black Americans and other Americans of color need to have economic institutions of their own to fall back on; that is to say, businesses of their own. Our social and economic lives just won't make sense until that happens.

I think this has to happen not just for pride, not just for the sake of making a contribution to the national economy, but for other reasons. A story that I always like to tell is about my great-uncle. It never really dawned on me just how important a man he was until after he died. In the '20s as a young man, he left South Carolina and moved to the city that became my home town — Evanston, Illinois. He started a milk company and delivered to the black community, but the business failed in the Depression. So then, he started a construction company, the Johnson Construction Company, and over many years, he built residences and apartment buildings and churches in Evanston. Across from my grandmother's house is a church he built, the Springfield Baptist Church. I saw these places he'd built as I was growing up but they didn't mean anything to me. Great Uncle Will was a contractor; it was his job.

But the reason my father came north from South Carolina in the '40s — from the farm he grew up on with five brothers and six sisters — was he needed a job, and my Uncle Will hired him, as he did my father's brothers. When they came north, there was a job waiting for them. Because of that, they were able to branch off, get other jobs on their own. That's a very important thing, the family business, that kind of economic self-sufficiency. It's the sort of thing you find in other communities as well, Jewish communities, Asian communities. You take care of your own, because the federal government is not going to do it. You can't ask the government to do it, because it's not empowered to do that.

There are certain things the government can do, like redress grievances and Jim Crow things that have been on the books for 100 years or more. The government can eliminate those and create open doors so there is no discrimination. But that economic center, that taking care of your own, is important.

Truth of the matter is the Nationalists believe in it; the Nation of Islam has always believed black people should own their own businesses. Ownership becomes power, because ownership mean independence. You can go to the negotiating table as an independent person, as the employer, not someone who is always the employee. You

can produce goods and services for others, just as everybody else does. You don't have to ask anybody for anything. Then you really are free. When people meet and they don't have to ask, to beg each other for something, then they meet as equals.

AH: You say that people aren't really free until they can meet as equals, but that seems to mean equals in the business sense. How do people achieve equality in the other arenas of life?

CJ: You know, it dawned on me — I've always known this, but it really hit me now in a serious way as a clear thought — that males and females in general have separate cultures. I mean there is a culture of women that is different than the culture of men, particularly when you're younger. I was thinking about this with respect to mothers, grandmothers, and daughters who get together in the kitchen after a meal and talk and there are no men around. Very often the discussion is about men and especially about the men in the family, and you can tell this because when a man walks into the room, the conversation changes. That kind of get-together offers a place to air questions and get positive support.

Well, young men have a similar culture, but it's not always positive. To the contrary, it's very often competitive and disruptive. I think that's one of the symptoms we see with gang behavior in general, but specifically in terms of young black males. Young men have those places where they go and do things together, where they talk about girls and let loose, as women do, and say outrageous things that they would never say in mixed company. It's a way of letting off steam and a way of gauging what you're doing in terms of your gender.

But they are two separate cultures, and the differences between them seem to be more pronounced right now. Or maybe we're just more aware of those separate cultures than we have been before.

AH: What are the consequences of that, I mean the differences between male culture and female culture?

CJ: We know some figures for young black males between 16 and 24 — the highest death rate in the country and the greatest cause of that high rate is murder. We know that one in four young black males is controlled by the penal institutions or the courts or the parole organizations. As a group, young black males have been hit very hard. I think about that a lot, because I have a 17 year-old son and we've talked a great deal about the kinds of pressure he has to face in the public school, for example, and from other kids. The fact is, if you're young, black, and male right now, it's hard to negotiate your way

through the social world, much harder than it was when I was young, 17 and 18 years old.

The facts about young black females are different, but the figures say over 50 percent of the babies born in black households today are born to single parents, leaving the woman alone with the baby, raising it herself. I don't think that makes it any easier for young black women.

AH: Politicians these days talk a lot about family values, or the lack of them, in modern American culture. How do those things you talked about — the high number of deaths of young black men from murder, the high percentage of black children born into single parent households — play out at home?

CJ: There are a lot of conflicts in the black home. Suppose, for example, you've got a young girl who gets pregnant and the boy is still a boy, not a man, and he doesn't want to get married. So the girl has to raise the child by herself, maybe along with her mother. And it becomes the mother's burden — she's raising her grandchildren as well as her children. Suppose the child is a male. He grows up, looks around. There's no father. His mother and grandmother can't watch him all the time — they're at work, right? So what does he do? He finds a support group he needs and the male models he needs outside, on the street, with other young males coming from similar situations. With no father at home, a gang offers structure — that's a powerful attraction. And what can black women, the grandmother and the mother, do in that situation? Well, they just have to wring their hands because they have done everything they could. They took him to church as a young boy, they've done everything possible. But because the father figure is not in the home to provide at least an alternative model to what is going on in economically depressed communities, where crime might be a way of survival, the situation at home will reach a point where the boy is going to break away.

But let's look at this a different way. Here is a figure I always like to point out: if one out of four young black males is controlled by the criminal justice system, that means that three out of four are not. And my question is: how did the three out of four manage to avoid that trap, that pitfall? There are black parents successfully raising their children and doing a very good job of it, but they don't get in the papers very often because it is not a national problem that they are doing their job.

The national problem is those young men who go from the street to prison and back to the street again. It's really a serious situation, and it's not going to go away. We're talking about an entire generation of young black males. Jesse Jackson points out there are more young black males in prison than going to college. That's serious.

AH: But is there anything that can done about it? What do you want to do about the situation?

CJ: As an artist, my thought is simply this: I think I should give — if I can rise to the occasion — not just to black people but to readers in general, the very finest art I possibly can. That's what I'm oriented towards doing. My background is in journalism and philosophy, and what I try to do is create a kind of fiction that I hope brings some degree of — I hate to use the word — enlightenment, as well as entertainment to people.

I want people to know some things about black history. It's a history that's been marginalized, so they might not have known these things before. So, surely, clearly, I have a pedagogic purpose — to illuminate, to reveal, to disclose something that is shadowy. And I try to do that in most of the things that I write.

There are black nationalist writers who would say that no white person could ever understand their work. The great phrase the black nationalists use is: *It's a black thing, you wouldn't understand.* It's even on T-shirts. So, if a white critic hated a black writer's work, it had to be good for black people. To my way of thinking, that's a bizarre, mindless, frightening notion, because if you can't read and understand something I wrote because I'm black or I can't read and understand something you wrote because you're white, then we really have no basis for common understanding. If through language, through art, through expression, through communication, we can't create a center out of which epistemology or all our knowledge grows, then all we have are camps that can never connect, a Balkanized country.

I process things through philosophy. I believe in reason and I believe we all have a rational faculty that permits us to understand. I believe that in my heart of hearts. ✌

WOMAN OF THE BUS

Omar S. Castañeda

Because of her I have given up on the 1 train and even the A. I ride the 4 bus now from Washington Heights to the 104 and down to 5th Ave. It is slow slow yet I have watched that woman ride the bus. I have seen her turn, Chekhovian, one supple calf raised, her ankle a sudden blossom of lines, her hand curving brilliantly around the rail. Bright silver railings, catching light. You see the flash that is forever burned into *nous*. So I have given up on the infernally bad 1. I let loose the blessed A. Watch her skirt just behind her knees. Wish my mouth at that juncture.

She ascends at any of several stops near Columbia-Presbyterian. Me: the Cloisters. The weather can be anything at all, it doesn't matter. Birds, exact clothes? Name them yourself. For I have seen that woman of the bus. I have descended as early as the George Washington Bridge to run along Ft. Washington in hopes of watching her climb the steel stairs, snap open her purse and toy with that coin eater. I have stood close enough to smell the sweat of her toil way uptown. It is a hyacinth on her shoulder. I have grazed my forearm to help her lift a bundle to the overhead. And in her quick crossing of legs, I have seen an obsidian sea that mocked the white stars above and suspended a moon neither sea nor star but blue and frightened like me.

"Woman of the bus, I have watched you."

"Get the fuck away from me."

She stares from the window, her palm inches from the glass so that in the evening reflection it is her eyes I see full of privacy. I wish the tip of my tongue within her life-lines, between her ammoniated fingers.

"I wish your tired hands would work just a little more with me."

"Creep!"

By now all the women are staring, the men with warning eyes. She shifts away and her sleeveless blouse opens beneath her arm.

"There is the hint of islands."

She moves to a farther seat. A large black man standing by the rear exit turns sideways in the aisle to block me from moving near her.

"Wait! Please! I have come here and wished I could rest my face in your hands. I know the very dirt you work in! I watch you look out over the city. You have sad eyes. You have crows in your head that fly out over everything. God, I've wanted you to dip your hands into my belly and let your blackness run like ink into my veins. Don't you see? I want you to dye my moonflesh, you to love me."

The black man peers at her. The women peer at me.

She jabs her finger against the black band so the driver will stop.

"I have pale eyes for you!"

This time there is nothing I want that happens. Oh, perhaps a shattering of ice, the tiniest of chips from some granite wall.

"Don't worry yourself for the woman."

"I have pale eyes for her."

The man looks down at his feet as I leave the bus. He moves a little so that I think he will console my shoulder, but he does not.

I do not go on the bus for two days. For two days I eat nothing but purple onions purchased from a Dominican man by St. Nicholas and 265th. I pass him after I mail a letter addressed simply to "Woman Of The Bus; #4; NYC 10032." It costs me $0.65 because I use a 6X9, No. 55 envelope with metal clasp and there are five heavy sheets of paper folded in half. I write a sentence on each sheet:

"Your arms hold a continent of dreams."

"Coconuts surround the world, ignoring the barriers of water, of land, of strife."

"The buttons of your blouse belong in my mouth."

"You might have turned me to ash."

"You might have turned me to ash."

My stomach enters into battle with me and I give up the onions. I eat two bunches of cilantro, chopped and spread among all the slices of a loaf of Wonderbread and go to sleep. In the morning I run in Fort Tyron Park so that my bowels will move. I eat a good lunch of Ethiopian *full* at the Red Sea on 125th and Broadway, under the shadow of the elevated 1 track. I pick up the 4 and will ride it until she appears if it takes all of eternity. I don't care.

When she appears I get on my knees in the aisle.

"For two days I have thought only of you. My head is completely filled with the horizons of your evenings."

"Boy, you the biggest fool. Why you come to me like this? Why?"

I take off my shirt so that she can see the answer in my flesh. I take off my pants, my shoes and socks. I take off my underwear.

"The poor chi-el in love."

"He a damn fool."

The other women shake their heads. They come closer to me.

"He love you."

She turns away and presses her dark face against the oily window-pane.

"Don't you know I do nothing but work? I ain't got time for playing no games."

One of the women has no teeth. She guides me from my knees and makes me sit on the edge of the seat. Her hands are like cherry root. She cradles my scrotum, measuring. The other women surround me.

"Why he doing this? Why?"

"He helpless. He poor and in love. He like a boat gone way away from home, now."

The toothless woman squeezes my dickhead so that the blood swells in the capillaries. She measures the length of my erection by using the old dents in her gums. She wiggles her hands side to side as if to say it is all right. Then she opens her mouth wide so she can use it to measure the girth of my testicles.

"He okay underneath."

"He love you, girl."

She looks at me now. The other women urge her to smile at me. My heart is beating so fast that my erection falls. A different woman reaches down and inserts her finger into my rectum. She teases my prostrate so the blood comes back.

"Look how he love you."

Toothless pinches Woman Of The Bus hard above the elbow.

"You take him home. No more a this stuff."

All of them guide her to me. I get back down on my knees. I slowly press my face into her crotch. Even through the skirt I can smell the perfume of hurricanes, of mountains. I cannot help myself. I begin to cry.

"Okay."

As I leave, the driver gives me my transfer.

"Thank you."

Everything is black. Our perspiration. Our breath. The heat from our bodies. The friction between us. So that I cry again and she takes me up with her arms and kisses each of my eyes.

"You making one hell of a burden on me."

I can hardly speak because of my crying.

"It's really you."

"Sure, ah-hum. Never mind. We see."

Woman Of The Bus leans back on the bed and opens her thighs again. This time I go in all the way until I am safely positioned inside her womb. Her legs close over me and all the light is gone. Black the amniotic sea. Black the heartbeat of my mother. Black the umbilicus now, crackling with something no white woman can ever possess. No stars here, no frightened moon. Only the rocking of ancient waters. Only the tides of life slapping ships burdened with dark cargo. Around me the clattering of metal links. Something old trying to deny itself. Something of betrayal and shame.

Inside her I feed on the ancestry of lions, the heritage of antelope. Always I hear the drumming of ships. The panther of her lungs purrs into me. Her claws scratch slowly the membranes of my ears, her blood delicious in my mouth, so that I do not ever want to leave the black warmth of her womb.

But she, riding the bus, breaks water and licks me clean. In her breasts again, I suckle from her tamarind nipples a fountain of marrow.

"Burden, like I say."

"No."

"What you want?"

"I want all women to be black as my wife."

"Wife!"

"I want them all to be night travelers."

"Boy, I done took the stars from your life and that sad little moon you was and now you want me to dip into the whole blessed world, too. Burden!"

I shake my head.

"You got legs, don't you."

"Please. Don't make me go."

"It's got to be this way."

She holds me and licks my hair until it is soaked and flat against my skull.

"You still white."

"Please."

I try to catch the eyes of the other women on the bus, but they all turn away. Even Toothless.

"I love you."

"You loves truth. An decency, I gives you that, but I never be your wife. If I anything I be your mama."

The other women nod when I look at them. Toothless stands up. She is old old.

"Go on now."

"It's got to be."

I take out my penis for them, but they shake their heads.

Toothless says, "Time be done for that, boy. Go on use it uptown an downtown so's you do your mama proud. But don't you be shaking it here. A boy ain't a man till he leave home."

"Come here."

I move to her.

Woman Of The Bus kisses me on the forehead. Her heart is oil, covering me, seeping into my pores to drench the insides of my body.

"Warrior. Black warrior," she whispers.

Toothless nods beside her.

"Your weapon be that shallow white skin."

"Yeah? Where I go?"

Toothless smiles. "Now you be right."

"Live on an fight," Woman Of The Bus says. "Be a guerrilla."

She gives me the power sign.

"Yeah," I say. "Okay." ✐

© 1988 *Childhood is Hell* by Matt Groening. All Rights Reserved. Reprinted by permission of Panthon Books, a division of Random House, NY.

About the origins of language and tribes little is known, though they do seem to be roughly coincident historically. It's a chicken-and-egg question among some anthropologists whether one made the other possible, or vice versa. Similarly, the invention of writing is related in time to the breakdown of "primitive" societ-

> *this tribe believes there are those among us who would become angels*
>
> *later we see them on television & they are ghosts we would have loved to have known*
>
> *had we known what 'love' meant, or 'angel', or 'ghost', or 'tribe'.*
>
> ANSELM HOLLO

ies and the rise of civilization, of cities, nations, and states. From Confucius to Orwell, we know that the moral order of our social structures is dependent upon the clarity of language both spoken and written. These days, some 100,000 years after *homo sapiens sapiens*, Man the Double Wise, started talking about getting together for the common good, bonding ragtag bands of hunter-gatherers into larger groups called tribes, the chatter goes on, a lot of it, ironically, about "tribes," most of it by white people looking for a way out of their paradise lost. It's a measure of our desperation that we seldom know what we're talking about.

From Rousseau's Noble Savage to '60s-inspired freak show "Gatherings of the Tribes"; from Thoreau to *Dances with Wolves*; from poet Charles Olson to the recent 10-part PBS series *Millennium: Tribal Wisdom and the Modern World*; from little boys who really played "Indians" when they played "Cowboys and Indians" to "white tribalism" eco-guerrillas in the northwest forests; from 30-something drumming circles to an *Utne Reader* spin off called "On the Importance of Being Tribal and the Prospects for Creating Multicultural Community" — it's an industry.

The more that's said about "tribes," however enlightened or well-intended, the more confused I get. Reading in *The New York Review of Books*, I come across the claim of a British literary critic that American poet John Ashbery is "major" because he has "changed the language of his tribe." Reading in *Harper's*, I come across a confession by an urban white guy in a three-piece suit who feels better now that he carries a spear around town.

The word has come to mean everything to everybody, and there are books to prove it. Take *Tribes*, a terrible 1988 quasi coffee-table production by hedgehog-idea-man Desmond Morris, who's fooled millions with such classics as *The Naked Ape* and *Babywatching*. Filling his text with colorful photographs — a la *The National Geographic* — as proof, Morris, essaying that "Man is a tribal animal," seems bent on demonstrating that this is true from Borneo to Boston. Borneo makes sense. But Boston?

Morris's white people are so tribal that they live in a K-Mart of social and cultural associations — from Elks Clubbers to rock fans, the Army, class, church, political parties, softball teams, the corner tavern, whatever. Because all people everywhere bond together in groups of which the glue is ritual and tradition, then all is tribal. This line of reasoning makes it possible for someone in this country to be a member of five or six different tribes, all at the same time. Just sign on the dotted line.

Morris isn't bothered by the fact that none in this multitude of postindustrial tribes ever link up to a larger purpose, such as the common good. More interested in superficial similarities between indigenous people and their high-tech counterparts, he ignores the fact that, however tribal the latter might look or behave, they lack everything in substance: ancestry, the generational handing down of knowledge, roots, identity with their first and formative culture, a wholeness of soul. In a chapter called "Emblems of Allegiance" Morris sets portraits of two young men side by side. One is an Indian, relatively untouched by civilization, who squats in the jungle, staring into the camera, his cheek tattooed, his head half-shaved to support a red and white mud cap that sports orange, yellow and green plumage. The other, similarly posed, like a twin, is a white punk rocker in a dirty city, glaring at the camera, who wears an earring and has an eagle and an anarchist symbol tattooed on his shaved head, which is crowned by a bright red mohawk.

Which is where the comparison has to end, if "tribe" or "tribal" is

to mean anything at all. What does it mean to suggest that the largest tribe in the world is alienated white youth? Whatever his outward trappings, in all other psychological respects the punk is no more "tribal" than the Indian is a nobody lost in the city. One vessel is empty, the other full. They are different orders of consciousness. One is alone in a crowd, with little sense of past and less of future, the present a drag, living outside of Nature, the other is integrated with all creation, secure in family and friends, past, present, future, ritual and tradition.

This kind of confusion seems pervasive to me in the so-called majority culture dialogue about "tribes" and "tribal wisdom." For instance, with respect to the *Utne Reader* mentioned above, I always thought "tribe" and "community" were two different concepts. Factor "multicultural" into the equation and they come out opposites. In the history of our evolution as social beings, tribes are the beginning of hierarchy, status and difference. Few are willing to talk about this. From the perspective of Anthropology 101, tribes are characterized by a common name and language, contiguous territories, similar cultural behavior, a tradition of ancestral descent and continuity, and decentralized political control entirely in the hands of men. There is a sense in which to say tribal bonding is to say male bonding, or at least hunter/warrior bonding. This is a working or operative definition of what scientists mean when they say "tribe," though they would acknowledge the term's exceptions and ambiguities.

More subjectively, tribes have come to symbolize a way of life that offers belonging, home, individuality instead of individualism, harmony with Nature, a cure for whatever ails the modern spirit. Afraid, neurotic, disgusted with the "civilization" that's grown up around us, we talk about "tribes," hoping to find in their example a way to fix the future.

I sympathize. I suffer the same fear, night sweats, rage, and disgust. But I have severe doubts that a whole lot of white people talking about tribes will ever ease our condition. For one thing, it avoids the real issue, which is white culture and the brink it's brought us to. We don't understand ourselves, and we never will, genuinely, until we pay as much attention to our own tribal beginnings as we do to others'. Somewhere along the line we have to understand that the culture we want to change is linked by a process of evolution to *our* tribal heritage, a cold-weather outlook different than that of a Trobriand Islander.

There's more than irony in the fact that "tribe" is from *tribus*, the

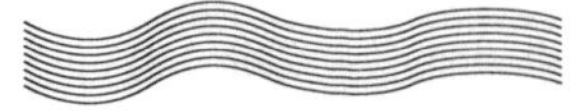

Roman word for the herds of people who wandered outside the imperial city gates. On the basis of what's taught in our schools, it's easy to see that white people don't have a tribal history of their own, an understanding, that goes deeper than the Greeks (or Jean Auel's *Clan of the Cave Bear*). Maybe that's one reason we're always running off to be black, red, yellow or brown, colonizing other cultures, turning Chuck Berry into Pat Boone, eastern religions into western business strategies, and Native American mythical critters such as Coyote into ready-made pets for white poets, essayists and storytellers to wax grandiloquent about.

When white people think "tribe," what image fills their mind's eye? I'd wager more see a teepee than a stone house in Scotland — or a turf and fur-covered dwelling built on bare Ukrainian steppes 15,000 years ago, 16-feet in diameter, each framed out of 23 tons of mammoth bones. I bet more see a totem pole than a dolmen stone. Because we don't know who we are, I'd also bet we'd imagine Apaches or Amazonian Indians, rather than Angles, Jutes, Saxons, Kelts, Slavs, Finns, Teutons, Goths, Vandals, Croats, Serbs, or dozens of others that form the European tribal epoch from which we sprang. Mesolithic forest folk. Early Neolithic farmer-settlers. Veterans of four Ice Ages, getting ready to conquer the world.

This is not some plea for "White History Week," nor the beginnings of a separatist tract. The fact is that one can go to the library in search of books about these white tribes and find but a few. (Three good ones include *The Europeans*, by John Geipel, Stanley Diamond's *The Search for the Primitive*, and Henri Breuil and Raymond Lantier's *The Men of the Old Stone Age*.) Part of the reason, surely, is that a few bones and artifacts can't tell us a lot. Also, it's more fun to go to a jungle and study a living tribe, which we then kill as we dissect, convinced that we, too, were once whole and wise.

But this can't account for the want of information, however speculative, about the social and spiritual temperament of the white tribes whose cultural progress has wrought global havoc. The question has nothing to do with the history of science and ideas. It's not how or when we came to model our universe on the triangle rather than the sphere, but why. Knowing next to nothing about the origins of culture and the dawn of consciousness, we make the mistake of assuming that the study of today's indigenous peoples will help to clarify these matters for us, personally.

We don't understand ourselves. James Baldwin once put it this way: "The

really ghastly thing about trying to convey to a white man the reality of the Negro experience has nothing to do with the fact of color, but has to do with this man's relationship to his own life. He will face in your life only what he is willing to face in his own." David Mura, in a tiny paragraph in said *Utne Reader*, writes: "Whites must see the problem of race as one of giving up power…. Whites need to admit that their understanding of the lives of people of color is limited, and that limited knowledge has allowed them to feel comfortable with the status quo. In short, whites need to listen." Wanda Coleman, in a piece about Thelonious Monk in *Caliban* called "On Theloniousism," rails against the "fashionistic cannibalization" of black culture by whites with an incisive eloquence that says it once for all.

I could cite many other such criticisms. Whenever non-whites are given a chance to answer the question "What should whites do?" they invariably respond: shut-up, listen, try to figure out who you are, where you came from, and why all this greed and violence. To which white people say cool and traipse off to have a shamanic experience or write articles called "The Boomers' Search for Community: Is It True Community or Tribal Networking?" Meanwhile Leonard Peltier rots in a federal prison, the David Sohappy family is destroyed, peyote-eating Native Americans are made criminals, and the U.S. government declares it has the right to decide when a tribe becomes extinct.

Another pernicious aspect of this confused talk about tribes is that we only see and discuss one-half of the social organism: the "good" side, the potlatch side, the side that lives in communion with Nature, etc. What's overlooked in this celebration of values is that the social structure that gives them life runs counter to the Western humanist tradition — by which I don't mean to defend the latter. I only wish to point out that a tribe doesn't have any use for values such as liberty and civil rights. Nor for women's equality, an issue that is largely rationalized away by saying that, well, at least within a tribe women have themselves — a tribe within a tribe? — a sense of belonging and a sense of purpose. Not to mention foot-binding, clitirodectomies, and female infanticide. Tribes are built on custom, not laws.

Also linked to these troubling questions is the idea of difference, upon which tribes are based. Differences are the ties that bind — "they" don't talk like "us," look like us, eat like us, etc., therefore it's all for one and one for all and damn the rest. Formed around common interests, tribal structures *politicize* xenophobia. This is "tribal wisdom," too. To build in rootless, multicultural modern society a just social structure based on mutuality and the common

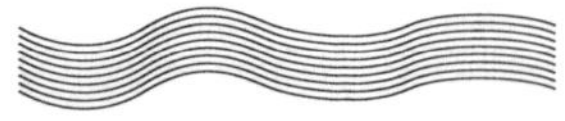

good, without patriarchy, status, and group unity based in part on fear of others, is to create something quite unlike a tribe, for which the word has yet to be invented, though commune comes close.

Likewise, that we see in tribal life the virtues of decentralized government doesn't mean that the model is at all applicable to mass urban society that initially broke with tribal consciousness 3,500 to 7,000 years ago. Plato's *Republic* can be read as a recognition of this break and the first defense of a "civilization," of a way of life that every major thinker since has come to disavow and criticize. Something in us snapped once tribes grew into nations and nations into states. (The first recorded suicide, that of Saul in the *Old Testament*, occurred around this time.) We can't just revert to animism and gift relations overnight, even if we feel their psychic loss like an amputee a missing limb. Those spiritual and social mind-sets often sentimentally referred to as "the old ways" can't be willed into existence. Anything less is nostalgia. We need new words, new ways.

Until then, the more nostalgic we become, the more self-deluded and vicarious, the further removed we get from the fact that we live in a multi-national corporate market economy ostensibly controlled by nation-states, as opposed to an ecological economy held in common. More appalling is the fact that consumerism feeds on a "tribally" factionalized society, marketing all the costumery, brand names, foodstuffs needed to assure one's allegiance to this or that group. The idea that state-capitalism is compatible with tribalism, or that hundreds of unrelated tribes can exist within it, like subcultural tapeworms feeding deep in the bowels of consumerism, is silly.

None of this is to say that "tribal wisdom" doesn't exist, or that our tribal origins aren't existential facts of the modern condition. Nor is this a call to abandon the "primitive," to forget about selectively incorporating the wisdom of "primitive" cultures into our own. The rub is that in order to do so in a manner that is concrete rather than abstract, will require nothing less than a transformation of Western thought and power structures. In preparing ourselves for this task, it might be more constructive if we rediscovered our own tribal origins: Druids and Hindu Brahmins rather than Black Elk, the Caves of Lascaux rather than She Who Watches, European megalithic religions rather than Native American creation myths. Failing this most basic understanding of ourselves, the roots of our barbaric and plundering ways, my hunch is that we'll go on play-acting Indians until all the Indians are dead, not to mention the planet. ❧

BARK US ALL BOW-WOWS OF FOLLY

Ken Kesey

It was past eleven by the time they reached the Dog House. The crowd had stopped its grumbling and was standing silent, faces turned toward the extreme northwest. They were watching the sun squeeze out of the belly of a tight little black cloud nesting on the horizon, like an egg squeezing out of a hen. The faces all turned when the van pulled into the president's parking space alongside the packed porch. No one spoke, but a strange whimpering started up as the vice-president got out. Greer took the first glass held out to him and gulped it down without tasting what it was. Ike could not believe the size of the crowd. Men he hadn't seen around town in years were pumping Greer's hand and giving him the high paw. It looked like every dunk and duffer that had ever shelled out the fifty bucks for the membership card had made his way to the meeting. He saw some that must have flown in from chapters as far as Anchorage to the east and Unalaska to the west.

Greer slipped alongside of Wayne Altenhoffen. "Still no sign of Billy?" he inquired in a hollow whisper.

"Nary a yip," Altenhoffen whispered back. "The Squid isn't one to cut short a shopping trip, even if he's heard of this movie shindig. So you're our prez tonight, Emil. You're the man with the plan. What are the Dogs going to *do*?"

Greer lifted his bony shoulders in a feeble show of nonchalance. "About what, Poor Brain?"

"About us getting sniffed over like this! Not Dog One has received an invitation to this high roll on the yacht tomorrow. That constitutes a gauntlet slap to our collective muzzle, wouldn't you say? Underdog honor is at stake, Brother Greer, and as fate would have it you are the man. So what's the plan?"

Other members were pressing close to the whispering pair.

"The plan is," Greer put on his shades and turned toward the horizon, as ceremoniously as he was able, "to wait until the sun goes

down, then have our meeting. Just like always."

The sun neared the horizon and the crowd began to quiet. Even the desultory whimpering ceased, except among some of the mascots. These malcontents were dragged away to their respective pickups and tethered there, downcast and ashamed but still unable to curb their whining. The smaller, more civilized dogs were herded beneath the porch, where they watched in decorous silence through the latticework. As the sun touched the distant line of water, even the whiners in the pickups became completely silent. When the last red blob spread out and blinked to green, a terrific howling ululation commenced, perfectly on cue. The effect seemed somewhat burlesque at first, self-mocking and more than a little shallow, but as the howling lifted there were heard notes of true pathos beneath the parody, of honest achings and deep animal despair being given throat, and the self-consciousness and the burlesque melted, and the shallow was swept into the deep. The obedient and the civilized beneath the porch joined in with a sweet tenor, then the heartbreaking baritone from the pickups. These notes spun and twined and plaited into a line of surprising strength — a single sobbing wail: the Call of the Underdog. This wail continued until it lifted above the town and rebounded off the face of the little glacier across the bay and came echoing back, reweaving with itself like the chord of a pipe organ in a vast cathedral. When the echo died away the men began to file into the hall, leaving cans and bottles and fruit jars outside in the brimming trash barrels — another rule learned from experience.

Not a word was spoken as card tables were swept clear and folded against the walls. Wooden chairs were dragged from closets and unfolded in uneven rows around the wooden floor. When every member was standing in front of a chair, Greer walked stiffly to the big cutout of the hydrant logo that served as the podium. He raised the polished bear femur that represented the chief's gavel and with his other hand pointed a finger at the floor. "Sit," he commanded. They sat. He held the hand up, palm toward the multitude, and bade them "Stay." His voice was steady. They stayed. "This Midsummer Night's Full Moon Howl of the Loyal Order of the Underdogs is now in session. Have a care and govern yourselves accordingly. Faithful Scribe, Poor Brain? Is there any old business?"

Wayne Altenhoffen stood up with a black ledger and opened it with a flourish. Altenhoffen was a substitute teacher at the high school when he wasn't fishing, as well as the editor of the *Kuinak Bay Beacon*, the town's weekly or biweekly or sometimes bimonthly

news rag. Long-nosed and wordy, he was nonetheless a valuable asset to the town and the club both, a bright and eager citizen who was often so full of plans for community productions and projects that he would begin a conversation: "My poor brain is simply *pulsating* with possibilities."

"The previous meeting of the Loyal Order ended on a sudden and dramatic note," Altenhoffen read. "The matter before the members was the court order to cease and desist the practice of setting off fireworks in the meeting hall. When informed that Thomas Toogiak Senior and the Searaven council had threatened to evict our organization, President Squid stated, and I quote, 'Fuck Tommy Toogiak and his whole band of beer-barrel savages. If they mess with the Dogs I'll cut off their tea cold turkey. We shall set off firecrackers when the spirit moves us.' Unquote. Members agreed with a unanimous woof except for Tommy Toogiak Junior, who objected to his father being cursed, and Charlie Fishpool who objected to some of the other wording. 'Beer barrels we may be but savages we ain't. We are *descendants* of savages.' Norman Wong responded, and I quote, 'Then descend back to your seat, Charlie; your beer barrel's showing.' To which Charlie Fishpool responded, 'At least I descend from somebody, Wong.' At which point Brother Norman Wong struck Charlie in the back of the neck with a rolled-up *People* magazine, knocking the aforementioned Charlie to his knees. Then Brother Clayton Fishpool struck Brother Norman Wong on the back of his neck with a rolled-up copy of *Atlantic Monthly*, knocking him to his knees. Then the meeting broke up."

He closed the book and raised his bright face. Greer nodded his approval. "Thank you, Scribe Altenhoffen. Does the pack concur with the record?"

The room answered in unison, "Woof woof!" Altenhoffen sat down.

"The minutes stand approved as read. Any further old business?" Greer peered around fiercely, feigning confidence. Charlie Fishpool raised a thick hand.

"I'd still like to get an apology on the record, but maybe this ain't the time —"

"Woof woof!" the members agreed and Charlie took down his hand.

"Any reports from any committees?"

A deep negative growl answered.

"Excellent." Greer gaveled the podium top in a neat rim-shot con-

clusion: thump-a-bam! "Is there any *new* business, then?" The big white bone was held high, waiting. "Eh?" Nobody seemed able to think of any new business.

At the rear of the room near the door, Dog Brother Isaak Sallas let his chair tip back to the wall and relaxed. Greer was going to do just fine, he saw, for all that trembling and trepidation. That was one thing about the Underdog ceremonies: they could be counted on to keep the members from taking any business too serious, old *or* new. Finally. Wayne Altenhoffen placed his ledger on the floor and raised his hand. Greer sighed heavily.

"The chair *again* recognizes Scribe Altenhoffen. What's on your mind, Poor Brain?"

Altenhoffen stood amid low growls. He raised a finger. "I shall be brief," he promised, then drew a deep breath. "Mr Vice-President...Dog Brothers...fellow citizens...I wish to raise the question for discussion, with consideration for the Order's historic involvement in so many memorable events of the glorious past —"

"Grrrr," warned the members. They were all too familiar with Poor Brain's wordy preambles.

"— the question being *this*,"he hurried on, "*how* do the Underdogs go about getting their righteous bite out of this forthcoming action film?"

"Woof, *woof*,"the members seconded.

Greer stroked his frizzled chin. "A very interesting question, Scribe. Is there any discussion? If not —"

"I got a even more interesting question!" someone interrupted from the other side of the room. "How do we common Dogs get a invitation to this party tomorrow night — like certain *other* brown-noses got?"

"You're out of line, Dog Brother — " Greer gaveled. He couldn't see who had spoken.

"Where do we get *in* line, Mr Vice-President?" another growled. "Out at Loop's pigsty?"

Greer tried to slide it past with his Gallic shrug. "Zuch is zee movie business —" but the members were no longer in the mood for comedy. Mrs Herb Tom stood up, her red-nailed finger aimed like a pistol.

"Greer, so far you are the only dude in Kuinak with suck enough to get on that floating smorgasbord. Don't say different, the whole town knows. What *we* want to know is what you've done about get-

ting your loyal Dog Brothers a little nibble, damn your skimpy black ass! Is this a first-class club or what? I for one didn't pay five hun to sit home and watch the rest of the world ridin' first class. I could've given the money to Herb if that was what I wanted; he could've bought a new dish. So —" Mrs Herb Tom raised a black leather purse and poked the red-nailed hand inside, very pointedly. "— what about it?"

Greer was looking a little worried. "Mrs Herb… Dog Brothers…I swear to you I *asked* about getting the club passes on board. But the couple that entertained me did not speak one word of English — just Russian or something — and I never did see Steubins."

Mrs Herb was not appeased. "What about your albino buddy? He sounds like a understanding sort, catches you humping his wife, then provides you with a couple of replacements?"

"Vanished below decks, Brother Mrs Herb, right after he turned us over to the Russians. Vanished below decks. I haven't seen him since. Dog's honor." The knot had returned to Greer's brow and his hands were beginning to shake. "I don't know this albino dude hardly any *any*way. Listen, everybody; Alice Carmody's the one you ought to hit on. She *is* his mother…"

They didn't even honor this suggestion with words, just the low growl.

Ike let his chair tip back to the floor. Silly kidsclub business notwithstanding, you always had to keep in mind that the kids at these meetings were fully grown and usually drunk and frequently strung out and, more often than not, armed. As president, he'd more than once had pistols pointed at him over some silly kidsclub business. And the previous year the peaceful little town of Kuinak had chalked up the third-highest handgun fatality per capita in the nation, just behind Houston, Texas, and Washington DC.

"Then hit on Ike Sallas!" Desperate, Greer pointed with his bone. "Ike spent time in *jail* with the son-of-a-bitch; all I do is spend time with his mother *wife*…"

The faces turned, flushed and twitchy. The first signs of scoot withdrawal. Even the women. Ike found himself remembering why he'd stopped coming to these fun-filled monthly meetings.

"What about it, Sallas?" Mrs Herb Tom demanded.

"Don't look at me. You didn't see any Slavic twinkies bringing me a silver card with *my* name on it."

"My name isn't on mine, either!" Greer cried. "I mean, I don't *have* no stinkin' card."

The Dogs were not placated. Some continued to glare at Isaak, some at Greer. The growl kept rising. For the third time in two days, Ike regretted leaving Teddy at home; then, as if the thought itself had touched a trigger, a gunshot boomed in the room. Norman Wong waved a .44 Colt revolver over his head, the fourteen-inch barrel drizzling smoke. The piece was an antique Civil War weapon, property of the Order. It was issued to the sergeant-at-arms at his inauguration, and was to be passed along. Norman had held both post and piece since the club's formalization. Luckily, he was the coolest-headed of the Wong boys, and had never used the weapon except procedurally.

"Order in the den," Norman spoke into the blast's aftermath. There was order. Firecrackers and Uzis were one thing, but a big .44 had the ring of historic authority. "This is a formal meeting. Have a care and govern yourselves accordingly!"

The crowd settled muttering into their wooden chairs, turning back to the podium. Greer showed his teeth and tried to arch his eyebrows into some show of Jamaican cool.

"The Squid will be back in a couple of days, O my Brothers," he reassured them. "He'll take care of us."

The low rumble commenced anew. "Billy the Squid don't have friends inside on this one, Mr Vice-President," Mrs Herb pointed out. "*You* do."

"Woof *woogh-h-h-f*."

Ike heard the rumble rising — questions, demands, accusations. He was reminded again of the sound he used to hear from the field workers, and from other places — in the barracks at El Toro, in the cells full of unsleeping men at the Sheriff's Honor Farm. The sound came from an ache so common that any low-rung group might have produced it, from the bottom of any social ladder. This wasn't any melodic howl of mutual Underdog blues; this was the dark and dangerous complaint of the *mad* underdog, of the left-out, the cheated, the long-toothed and empty-gutted. This was the universal growl of guys who had purchased the centerfold but didn't get the girl, of wives that had bought into the bubbles of daytime soap operas while life just got dirtier — this was the grumble of dreams being disappointed and glands being denied. What the crowd might do if that grumble kept growing to its uncharted end was anybody's guess.

Trapped at the front of the hall, Greer kept stammering one-liners and reassurances, but the growl kept getting louder. The Boswell sisters had joined Mrs Herb in a shrill caucus. Sergeant-at-Arms

Wong waved his big pistol and called again for order, but it was clearly past that. More members were beginning to rise wild-eyed from their chairs. Norman Wong waved his pistol; Greer hammered the bone gavel; the growl got more thunderous. Then, at the peak of the turmoil, all of the lights in the hall flared to sudden dark — as though by a signal — and the growl was overwhelmed by an ear-splitting crack of actual meteorological thunder.

That little black cloud had apparently moseyed on into town after finishing with the sun, to see what was up. It had actually considered the uproar at the Underdog hall for a few minutes, before the town's power station had captured its fancy in the next block. All those wires and insulators and diesel-driven generators! It tossed its single bolt into the seductive spread of machinery with a passion that made the earth move and welded a wheelbarrow against a metal piling. Satisfied, it began to unload its little load of rain before turning back out to sea.

The members had of course gone immediately still and respectfully silent. One thing you do learn, living on the low rung: respect such manifestations as come from on high, beyond the ladder — like the weather. High-rungers could afford insulation from such annoyances, but not low-rungers. They were at the mercy of such mysteries.

And they remained motionless and silent as the rain hammered down and the real dogs whined under the porch, for a shared mystical moment. Then the reserve generators kicked in and tame electricity returned to the light bulbs. It had taken no more than a fraction of a minute, but the effect on the Underdog meeting was enormous. The tension in the hall was reversed as instantaneously as switching a toggle from negative to positive. Nobody questioned it. Everyone was on their feet, laughing and jostling and pounding each other's back and giving the high paw. Ike found himself swept up in the surge of relief with all the rest.

Greer tossed the gavel into the podium and hopped down the stage, headed for the door. As far as the presiding prez was concerned, this meeting was undeniably over. He was stopped in his tracks before his hand found the door handle. There was someone on the other side of the gritty screen. And he stood there so paralyzed, with such a look of abject surprise and dismay, that the celebrating members took notice and began to calm down. When they at last quieted, a friendly purr came through the screen: "Hi, guys. Can a stranger enter the sacred den?"

Ordinarily, the Underdog Growl of Warning would have answered such a request, but the members were too spent; they could only stare at the shape beyond the screen. Greer finally shook himself from his trance.

"Sure, hey, why not? The meeting's adjourned, mon. Come on in." Greer flipped the latch and swung open the screen. "Dog Brothers, this is Nicholas Levertov."

Nicholas swept through into the glare of curious eyes. He was wearing cream-colored slacks and shirt, with a pastel peach overcoat draped over his big shoulders like a cloak. The prescription lenses covered his eyes and a thin chain held a gold crucifix at his throat. He's dressed to look like a stereotype of some Italian film mogul, Ike realized, right down to the floppy Fellini fedora.

"Gentlemen, I hope you will forgive this unseemly intrusion — hello, Isaak, don't I look spif? — but I could think of no other way to catch you all together."

"So, now you've caught us," Norman Wong said. "So now what?"

Norman didn't like the way Greer had flipped that latch so fast; it was the sergeant-at-arm's duty to decide when the den was open to the public.

"So I was just dropping this by, Big Fella." The white fingers flickered and a black card appeared. "That's what." He put it in Norm's holster, alongside the .44. "Also, these." A fan of cards fanned out from each hand. "Be so kind."

The cards were all generic, inscribed only "Noble Underdog" — but they were official invitations nonetheless, and for everybody. The very last card of the fan was handed with a flourish to Ike Sallas. When Ike started to protest that he wasn't much on parties anymore, the man leaned close, said a brief something in Ike's ear, then swirled back out the screen the way he'd come. The Dog Brothers stood on the porch and watched the limo bounce down the rutty rain-slick street.

"Who was that masked man?" Scribe Altenhoffen was the first to speak. "The Lone Stranger, or the Tooth Fairy?"

"I think it was the Tooth Fairy," Mrs Herb Tom judged, "The Lone Ranger woudn'a kissed Ike Sallas on the cheek like that." ❧

TRIBAL LIFE

Lawson Fusao Inada

We went through a petrified forest to get there. Chunks of stone-trees sprawled in the sand as we bumped and swayed slowly by. When we arrived at our destination, men on horseback topped a rise, coming down to greet us.

Here was a Navajo Nation summer camp — brush arbors, corrals, sheep, horses — a high plateau with mountains all around. Earlier that morning I was passing through on asphalt when two women in traditional dress waved me down. Their truck had overheated; they needed a ride.

As Agnes explained, they were getting supplies for "First Night," the first of three nights, a "healing ceremony" or "sing." Each event would be held at a different site in the mountains and reached by horseback. I drove, they sang — a soft melody, over and over. Red earth, blue sky, petrified.

Grandmother was kneeling at the fire. She looked me over with her one good eye, then poured me coffee from an enamel pot. Children, adults, elders were seated all over — on rocks, on the ground, in shade and sun — chatting, laughing, eating.

They didn't pay me much mind, which was fine with me. After all, they had things to plan and do, things I knew nothing about. And it was a delicious feeling, actually (along with the delicious food — hot fry bread, steaming coffee, sizzling mutton), to be so ignorant in their midst, so I just sat there, enjoying the day, enjoying their way.

After a while, Grandmother said something to Agnes. "Grandmother asks who you are, where you're from." (Up to then, I was simply "Lawson from Oregon," the driver with the foreign plates. They didn't pry, and neither did I. This question, though, was important.)

"Please tell her that my name is Inada, and that I am a Japanese from California." This got translated, perhaps the first time in the history of the world that "Inada" was spoken in Navajo. Grandmother immediately replied, with something of a smirk, a smile, and a hmph.

"Well, Grandmother says she doesn't know about all that. Grandmother says you're probably a Yazzie, maybe Delbert Yazzie's son, from up by Shiprock." I broke into a wide smile, and nodded, and Grandmother, smiling, nodded back. Then she continued.

"Grandmother says we would be honored to have you at 'First Night.' And she also thanks you for giving us a ride." We nodded, smiled. "Please tell Grandmother 'thank you' for the invitation and this wonderful food. The honor is mine."

Now, as far as I know, I'm still Fuzzy Inada's son, from Fresno. And because of that, I've been in many similar situations — tribal, with clan affiliations. I've been there all my life. I'll be there after death. Let me explain.

I've heard it said that the Japanese are one big tribe. Well, I don't know about that. It's a convenient generalization, but for the sake of convenience I'll stay with the generalization, because I do know this much: wherever, whenever we may meet, or simply encounter one another, there's something in the air between us, a spark of recognition that might be termed a tribal connection. To me, it's more of a *feeling* than anything, like meeting a relative, or even meeting an ancestor. It runs deep, this sense of our people.

It's also like meeting yourself. And when you meet yourself, you belong. Which means that, while being an individual, you are also a crowd.

Now I don't want to get mystical here (or deal with the Japanese mystique, whatever that's supposed to be); rather, what I'm talking about is no big deal, just the way it is, and maybe it's the same for everybody. (Or could be; after all, we all stem from tribal societies.) No, we're common as clay, regular as rain; nothing exotic or special about us.

Just history, pure and simple — lineage, legacy. It simply comes with the territory, and if you don't like it, you can do something about it. For instance, one of my students told me: "Yeah, you might say I'm a 'Japanese-American,' but back home in Idaho I'm just your basic redneck cowboy." Okay, good enough, dude. Or, from another student: "Yes, I am a woman from Japan, but I think of myself as an *artist* first — and from here I will go to Spain, to study painting."

Myself, I'll admit I haven't always liked being Japanese, and there are some Japanese I don't necessarily like. I've learned to live with it, even work at it by reading about a country where I've never been and I'm often surprised by how Japanese I really am: "Hello, I'm calling to inquire about your academic..." "Are you Japanese?" "Well, uh, sure. Are you?" "Yup. Now what did you want to know about..." "Hey, wait a minute, lady: Who are you? Where are you from?"

And then we're off and running — the customary procedure of sharing tribal and clan affiliations, and so on down the line... "No kidding? I'll be darned."

Let me do the same for you. A simple show and tell procedure — some places, some dates. And for the sake of convenience, let's just go back a ways to the petrified forest.

Dusk. Little summer breeze. Full moon rising. Stars. Birds. Insects. Scent of juniper, sage. Sand, earth. Way over there, in the mountains. Maybe that's the "First Night" campfire. Let's proceed striking sparks of recognition.

For starters, let's say these rocks over here are Japan. Close enough. My mother's clan, Saito, comes from, and is still in, Wakayama Prefecture, on the main island. Not all that far — walking distance — from Osaka and Kyoto, which means that her parents had a semi-urban experience, at least for the 19th Century. This other rock is the island of Kyushu, the south land, my father's clan being from Kumamoto Prefecture — the sticks. (Or the fields, since "Inada" means "Ricefield." You get the picture.)

Prefecture-of-origin is very important to us — causing nods of recognition, acknowledgement — because the lay of the land says something about who and how we are, in Japan or elsewhere. As a matter of fact, I could stop right here at these rocks, because they have my history and destiny written all over them.

But let's go over here, to America. (Down there, of course, is South America where there's more of us than here. And, naturally enough, my Brazilian clans speak Portuguese. And these little rocks are Hawaii where my Inada grandfather labored on a plantation, for passage to the mainland.)

More islands, right. This big flat one being Fresno (urban/Saito/ Fresno Fish Market, mother born in back of the store, 1912), and this big bumpy one being the greater San Jose region (rural/Inada/ sharecroppers, father born on the Pajaro River, Watsonville, 1910). These islands/prefectures are also very important (more nods), and my father is the chief of Fresno's Kumamoto Prefecture Association. Moreover, my clans and extended-clans are prominent in both places.

This is where I come in — Fresno, 1938. Not just a place, not just a date, and I'm not just a Sansei (third-generation), either. Rather, I'm an older Sansei, or a pre-war Sansei — and, once again, we could stop right here, because the facts of my birth say just about everything about me: history, destiny, character, personality, the whole prophecy.

Which is to say: I speak Japanese, have a Japanese name, and was in the camps. Moonlight isn't necessary to see, and feel, the meaning. It's written all over me, wherever I am.

And with the camps came, sure enough, more islands, and what might be termed re-tribalization. And I'd say living in a specific place with a related people constitutes tribal life. And with the camps came extremely significant designations and distinctions that are with us to this very day: "What camp were you in?" Or, as my great-grandchildren in the next century will say: "What camp were they in?"

In my case, my lineage and legacy includes three, and each camp was different and the same. So let's see. Where were we? Well, back over there, that's the Fresno Assembly Center, the county fairgrounds — an "instant" camp, a "pre-camp" camp, with an instant legacy. Now over there — that low-lying rock in the brush — that's Jerome Camp, in the Mississippi delta, the swamp of Arkansas.

And this smooth one where we're standing — with the sand on it, see? — is Amache Camp, in the Colorado desert, not all that far from here. While we're at it, let's let that little stone by your foot stand for Leupp, a "mini-camp" right here, on the Navajo Nation. (And, yes, we had major camps on other reservations; so you might say that it makes sense that the chief camps administrator went on to become chief of the Bureau of Indian Affairs, where he "re-deployed" his policy of "relocation." Which included, yes, "termination." Which reminds me. Down the ridge, in Europe, our relatives had base-camps in Italy, France, Germany, and some of them liberated a camp called Dachau.)

Well, enough of that. Speak your piece, if you want. These rocks aren't going anywhere. Otherwise, we can just mosey on down to camp. Or maybe even, whoa, saddle-up and head to "First Night." Follow the fire, those sparks of recognition.

Boy, listen to those coyotes. But, you know, I've had this feeling all along: We are not alone. ☙

THE MORE YOU TALK ABOUT
PEOPLE STARVING IN SOMALIA
THE LESS TIME WE HAVE
TO DISCUSS FAMILY VALUES.

Maggie Eht-Chillay lies on a couch, breath rattling from her heaving chest. Her son Henry is worried her lungs won't hold out this time and she will die from emphysema. She has taken no food in days and hasn't the strength to talk.

Bending over her, the prophet from Assumption Reserve holds her emaciated hand and speaks softly. He has traveled 170 kilometers to Meander River Reserve to bring comfort and pray for the ninety-year-old woman. Taking his drum from a white cloth bag, Alexis Seniantha beats it slowly. He sings about wanting to be

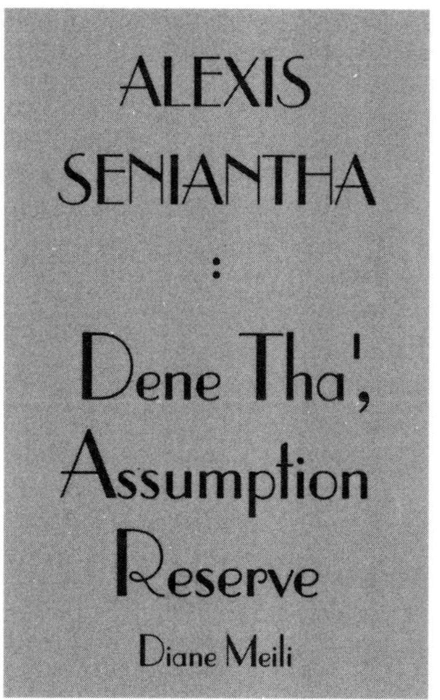

"where my Father's land is" and that "we are pitiful" on this earth.

"If something happens to us, our souls fly to heaven like a (prairie) chicken," Alexis assures Maggie. He sings another song, a more light-hearted one, then speaks again.

"You don't have anything to say about your future. There is a God and it's true. I saw my Father with my eyes."

Alexis's last song for Maggie is about Mother Earth and how God created the world for people. He explains his own mother once sang it for him, telling him to remember it in times of sickness. As the last drum beat fades, Alexis sets down his drum. Suddenly, Maggie struggles to sit up and begins talking. The strength in her voice astonishes Henry.

"Before, she couldn't even talk clearly!" he exclaims. Easily exhausted, Maggie thanks the prophet and lies back.

Henry tells Alexis that as a shy young man years ago he felt threatened by Alexis when the older man urged him to drum and sing for the people. "But now I see you're just an old man," he says. Henry is not being disrespectful. He is expressing his realization that Alexis is not to be feared. He is grateful to the kind elder who pushed him into becoming a shin Dene (song man). And although Henry is helping to keep the Dene tradition of praying with the drum and song alive, there are some who fear that when Alexis dies there will be no

one to take his place as a spiritual leader.

To the Dene Tha' (Ordinary People), Alexis is Ndátin — A Dreamer. He has developed a strong mind and lived a clean life. He can direct his dreams and receives messages from God. He is devoted to helping his people and, for years, has been the head prophet in Assumption, named the spiritual leader by Nógha (which means wolverine, pronounced No-ah), before he died in the 1930s. Dene Tha' in their seventies remember Nógha riding his horse around northern Alberta, conducting Tea Dances wherever he went, urging them to honor the Creator. Nógha received his power from wolverine, an animal portrayed in many Dene legends as being able to see things that are hidden. He looked into the future, and the old people who heard him forecast the changes to be brought by white newcomers say his words were true.

Alexis's granddaughter Molly Chisaakay says her grandfather was made a drumkeeper and was expected to follow a rigid code of ethics at a very young age.

"He felt he wasn't worthy. He had such a big responsibility. In spiritual leadership, it's not about how much you gain or lose, it's responsibility. When you take the drum, you have to be in tune with what it stands for. You have to live what you say about living a good and humble way by accepting the teachings of the drum. My grandfather could have drank alcohol when everyone else was, but he couldn't go against the teachings of the drum. But that's not to say he judges those who do."

As a child, Alexis listened carefully to his uncle Nógha's prophecies and to the advice of other elders. He heard over and over again stories about animal people and powerful ancestors who had performed heroic deeds. His senses were trained to detect information from the spirit world that went unnoticed by others. His elders told him it would be good for him to sleep beside a tree that had been split by lightning and touched by the Thunderbird if he wanted to seek his vision. Some children who became prophets had the ability to journey to heaven, and Alexis, now eighty-three, often speaks about his own spirit travels above the earth. He uses his hands expressively, grabbing his shoulders and shaking them when describing how he was thrown out of heaven.

"I was sick and just about died. If I put an offering in the fire for myself, I knew I might live. I wanted to know what's happening so I placed an offering in the fire. I started to sleep. I don't know what

happened. I must have gone to my Father's land. He saw me. 'What do you want over here?' He said.

"I said, 'I'm very tired and ill but I wanted to go to You.' He was smiling, looking at me.

"'Way down, people are pitiful. Work for them,' He said. I was grabbed and pushed out. There was nothing but blue sky. That's where I was set free. He's holding my arm. I went back to the earth. I was so thankful when I saw the world. My feet were together, on the ground again."

Before the dream ended, angels told Alexis where to find a moose on earth so he could hunt it.

"'Look over here,' I was told. I saw a cow moose. 'Hurry up to get that moose,' they told me. The moose won't go any farther, so just turn back[to get it],' they told me." Alexis describes how he woke up and felt better. His wife paddled him in a canoe to hunt the moose he had been shown.

"So all day, we went back. I could breathe good by then," he recalls. "So many difficulties and such a hard way of living. But when you've got to live, then you've got to live. It's not that difficult," Alexis says, referring to the help God provides to people who live straight lives.

"It is true there is a God, a Creator. He made the world for us. The clouds are high. That's where my Father's world is. It's very nice. But because I am here on earth, I'm going to help others."

Since Alexis has been to heaven in his dream, he has earned the right to direct Tea-Dance ceremonies for his people. Tea Dances are spiritual community celebrations for thanksgiving and socializing. Drummers, facing east, stand before a central fire within a fenced circle with openings to the north and south. Dancers move between the singers and the fire in a clockwise direction, the way the sun seems to move across the sky. The more footprints left in the Tea-Dance ring, the more the people move closer to God, the Dene say. The ceremony is a meaningful blending of Christian and Dene tradition, and the elders make no delineation between the two. For example, as men, women, and children place their tobacco offering on the fire, they kneel and solemnly touch their forehead, chest, and shoulders, making the sign of the cross on their bodies as Catholics do.

"There's a spiritual meaning behind everything at the Tea Dance," explains Molly. "The drum represents the circle of life. It's made of

an animal skin and wood, the Creator's gifts to us, and you have to heat it up near fire for it to sound good. There's a real power behind it. The drum brings people together and awakens something. When you hear it and dance, it's a way of expressing yourself, rejoicing. You realize you have this powerful connection between yourself, the Creator, and everyone else. If you're at a Tea Dance, you just don't want to sit down."

The Dene talk to the Creator with the drum which holds symbolic meaning, Molly says, and singing is an ancient practice. There are songs soliciting the Creator's blessing, honor songs for elders, women, and children, and some for different dances.

"A feeling can just well up from inside and you let it out, like you're crying for the people," Molly explains.

At Tea Dances, Alexis invites the people to pray, dance, share, and live clean lives. He wants them to look closer at life and concentrate on positives so they will fly straight to their Father's land when they die.

"It looks really nice there. There is no dirt in the land. There is tall grass, but it's not the same as here. The ends are sharp. It looks different. Like cattails. I saw it with my eyes. I thought it looked very beautiful."

Before the dancing begins, Alexis and other elders place tobacco and food offerings on the fire, then they may talk to the people about what they see coming ahead. Information about the availability of animals for hunting or the severity of the coming winter are just two examples of what they might share.

"I know my own journey and I am becoming more aware," Alexis tells his people. "Before I go to sleep I pray to the Creator. I see the pain in my people and feel it with my family. In my dream, I look ahead. What is going to happen? When I do look, I'm wondering if I'm going to be around to see what is going to happen. The angels tell me, 'You are going to stay as long as you can through tough times.'"

The ability to direct dreams and look ahead is a spiritual gift prophets have long used to help their people survive. Falling asleep, a person who has dreaming abilities can travel, in spirit, to locate animals in the bush. When the dreamer awakens, he or she describes the locations of the animals encountered in the dream, and the hunters go to those spots and make the kill. In the same way God showed Alexis where to find the moose, the dreamer helps his or her people

to find what they need spiritually, by relating God's messages to them and reminding them that an all-knowing creative force watches over them.

"At the Tea Dance, we pray. The people want me to talk. Even if I say something to them, they don't believe it. They'll see. Heeeeee! They'll wonder why they didn't change. I am taught everything. I know. This drinking business. The people think nobody sees them do bad things to each other. But if they die, they will see. They'll wish they obeyed the pitiful old man. I know it's very hard."

Alexis prays constantly for his people. "When I go to bed, I pray, then sleep. In the morning, I get up and pray again. After that I drink tea. I don't eat, I just drink tea. I look at what is happening. Why do people drink? I pray they won't do that. It should be quiet. They should just pray. Myself, I don't bother with liquor. Never once has liquor touched my mouth."

Alexis knows alcohol is the symptom of a larger problem. He realizes how complex the world has become with the impact of the dominant society. He mentions a simpler time when he was young and living off the land.

"We lived at Tu Lonh [Zama Lake, located west of Assumption]. I lived in a tent, but it's nice. We were heading farther and farther out with our traps. Out there, I killed three moose. Three cow moose. It's wonderful to be able to feed everyone, I thought. We went for furs. My traps were still set. We set camp for the night. At the next camp, I killed three moose — one fat cow and two young, quite big. Next morning, we started on our journey. We headed back for Zama Lake. I had good dogs, and our blankets, all our belongings were packed on the sled. We returned to our tent and I cut some of the wood and made a fire and went back out to work. When it got warm, I went inside."

Molly recalls the fascinating story her grandfather told her when she asked how he and her grandmother, Betsy Metchooyeah, became husband and wife.

"My grandmother was an orphan. She was a good trapper. She knew how to take care of herself. I think she was about twelve years old when my grandfather picked her. He brought her a whole load of gifts, and she was trying on the dresses and shoes, putting ribbons in her hair, putting on make-up, eating candy, just having fun. But when reality set in, she stopped to think, 'You're going to be married.' She stayed away for two days to think about it. When she came

back, she brought food. She said to my grandfather, 'This is my answer. We will have some nourishment and so our marriage will bear fruit.'

"My grandmother was small, but she stood her ground. She never said anything without good reason. She was a trapper and she told my grandfather she had her own ways and they must not go on each other's trapline or they might have accidents or arguments. She told him not to bring anything into it [the marriage] or there would be problems…just to bring himself and they would start their lives new, together."

Molly marvels at the maturity of her grandparents at such a young age. She says they lived together for two years without sexual relations until her grandmother began menstruating and underwent a period of isolation and ritual between "the earth and herself." After that, she had her first child.

"My grandfather told me they had a good life together. I think his parents taught him well. His mother told him, 'If you strike a woman, you have destroyed something.'"

Life in the early 1900s was simple but hard, Alexis admits. Death was always close by, and he recalls the sorrow he felt when his brother Billy died. He had been well respected by the people and once killed a grizzly bear that had been terrorizing the camp.

"One day, my brother went outside his house. As he walked back by the pile of sawdust, he just fell like that. When I got to where he was, I was shocked. I cried with all my heart. He had told me before not to cry, but I couldn't help it." Later, Alexis says he was confronted by his brother's spirit. "I looked inside his house. I saw him crawling in his house. He crawled a bit farther and got up. He said, 'Just like I told you before, I would fly like a grouse to heaven. Why are you holding me back?'" Alexis confirms the grief of the living can hold dead relatives and friends back from starting their journey to heaven, but when someone does make it safely to the other side they send a song back to earthly friends or relatives. The Dene say when this happens a person will receive a song in their sleep and, upon awakening, find it impossible to forget.

According to Nógha's prophecies, if the Dene people really listen to the messages and songs sent from heaven and pray with all their strength, they and the world will not be destroyed. The people must not let go of the traditions like placing tobacco on the fire and praying at Tea Dances. Alexis continues passing along these teachings and

is one of only four recognized elders in Assumption who speak about spiritual matters at gatherings.

As Molly notes, Alexis had a distinct personal way of teaching, too. "Elders tell stories in a general, simple, symbolic way. You have to translate it to your life situation. My grandfather has always told me to listen. When I would talk and talk about my problems, he would tell me to take time to be quiet and listen. I remember being outside and while I talked my grandfather chopped wood…never said anything. Then, he finally said something like, 'You can learn a lot from wood.' I think he was telling me to be quiet, like a piece of wood, or to concentrate on chopping it or something like that. Maybe I'd get an answer from inside myself, from my spirit, if I'd let it come. He never told me what to do.

"Some people think our elders are wishy-washy and should be more aggressive about stopping today's problems. But they cannot go against tradition and they never force things. They are trusting and almost innocent in that way. They are so spiritual, and some people have gone so far away from that, they can't understand any-more." Molly says her grandparents raised her in a way that developed her awareness and respect toward other living things which also have a spiritual life.

"We were out walking one day and I stepped on a flower. I said, 'I'm going to pick it,' but my grandmother told me to leave it.

"She said, 'Nature is strong. As we pass, it's going to open up again, so leave it alone. We're not here to destroy nature. The Creator cares about that flower.' At night, by the fire, she'd say, 'Look at the stars, then look at our fire. It's small and you can only see its sparks from a little ways away. But the stars, you can see their light forever. That's our Creator. That's how powerful He is.' When we left camp, we always made sure everything was left clean behind us."

Alexis speaks about God and tradition so people can make the choice to live fulfilling lives. He reminds them of Nógha's faultless vision and how he foresaw bad times, making it all the more impor-tant that they pray and stay true to their traditions.

Nógha spoke of "yellow papers" that would fool the people. Alexis believes these to be the government welfare checks that im-paired the work ethic once so critical to Dene survival. He predicted the land will be criss-crossed with lines, and the cut-lines slashed by oil companies that moved into the Assumption Reserve area not long ago have proved his words true. The prophet also foresaw strong

winds and speculated about "something terrible coming." He said the earth will not move because it is "tremendous," but things would move on the surface of the earth. Another of Nógha's prophecies states that "if you all forget to pray, then there will be no sun for a month. In the morning, the sun will rise, followed by the moon, and as they climb higher they will eclipse each other at noon. The sun will stop there, midway in its path, for one hour. Together, the sun and moon will set and there will be darkness."

Alexis grew up with the prophecies and knows the healing power of prayer. Many credit him with inspiring Dene in his own community and in places like Fort Rae and Fort Edzo in the Northwest Territories to revive their traditional Tea Dance religion.

"In fact," says Father Camille Piché, the Catholic priest at Assumption, "a little while ago, when Alexis was sick in the hospital in Edmonton, the people up north saw blood-red northern lights and they worried they were a sign that Alexis wasn't going to live much longer. Everyone thinks so much of the prophet."

Though Alexis may talk about apocalyptic times to come, he believes people will be safe if they pray for guidance on life's journey and treat the earth and each other with love and respect. He knows there are tremendous spiritual forces to help those who ask for assistance and stop hurting themselves and others. That is why he calls Tea Dances and finds the energy to attend meetings and gatherings, gently reminding the people to pray.

And as long as he is alive, they will. ❧

My essay is a Walkabout and an aside on the poetic process; specifically a meditation on two poems selected for the 1992 Seattle Metro Poetry Bus arts project. The poems were entered blind and naked, in company with a thousand other submissions. Blind and naked, an apt metaphor. This is the way we enter the world, with mother-mucous and blood in our eyes. We spend the rest of our lives on a Walkabout, trying to clear our vision; looking for the sacred stick or the magic stone to bring back to our totem clan. Let the reader go about his/her own perambulation with a text, divine the landscape first hand, before I leap from the rock and shake my turtle-shell rattle.

I

Walkabout

> It's after midnight.
> I'm trying to walk her out.
> An April rain nicks blossoms,
> Mashes them to a sweet paste.
> I scoop a handfull
> And plaster it on my shirt,
> Over my heart.

II

The poems are separated in Dream Time by two Aprils and were written for two women. The obsession with the one in Walkabout ended in a major clinical depression, autumn of 1990, and two hospitalizations in a psychiatric ward, where I met the second woman. Loony bins are full of wounded lovers, abused wives, and failed suicides who have come back for another try at living or a second suicide attempt: Life and Death; Eros and Thanatos. 69 and figure 8.

III

Welcome Back From a Suicide

> On your first walk outside the hospital
> Note the energy in each blossom muscle.

Trust there are many who love you,
And open your marvelous heart —
Clenched against fatherly blows.

There is a fierceness in flowering.
Stand beneath a plum
And hold out your arms.
Let light wash over your face
And pour into your palms.

IV

My two muses shall remain anonymous. We will not appear on the
Oprah Winfry Show to throw open our coats and show off hickies
or self-scarifications. The aim of such talk shows; the purpose of tele-
vision programming, is to tittillate a bored and soul-less society so
that its citizens may go shopping without guilt. To shop is the sad
metaphor of North American Present Time. It is the poet's thankless
task to strike the cultural set, to walk behind the soap opera scrim,
to burrow in the sheets and get mucous on your face — mucous and
semen, the primal stuff, the mess of love. To imagine being a Sphinx
Moth; plunge into a Desert Primrose; splash pollen all over thorax
and wings. Poets are emotion addicts and beauty junkies. Always in
need of a fix. Eros and self-knowledge occur in Dream Time. Our
culture has forgotten this.

V

In 1989 I fled high-rent California and moved back to the Pacific
Northwest. My tumble weed roots are in Eastern Washington, where
my father moved our family in 1944 to work at the Hanford Atomic
Engineering Works. A young woman, a journalist, had been at a po-
etry reading in Cazadero, California, when I read from *Black Ash,
Orange Fire*. She later moved to Washington and wrote me how
much she treasured my book. I looked her up and swept her off her
feet, *at first*. A truly Western Romance.

VI

If I seem to digress and wander, remember, I am on a Walkabout.
We males were sent on Walkabouts or into the *kiva*, to get away from
our mothers and to become men. Women are dangerous, magic,

powerful. The irony is that we must go on a journey to truly understand the power and depth of the Feminine. My feet are sore and raw, I've been walking a long time.

VII

Back to the Psych Ward. As one of my counselors joked, she was going to have T-shirts printed up with the words: MENTAL HEALTH MAKES ME SICK. I had my own T-Shirt idea: LOOKING FOR A WOMAN WHO HAD A HEALTHY RELATIONSHIP WITH HER FATHER. With an 800 number listed.

VIII

We have no rituals for getting well, for healing. No Sings or Sand Paintings or Walkabouts. We have, rather, bleak and sterile psychiatric wards. Many of the patients in these wards are victims of child or spousal abuse. The shrinks and skull-knockers do the best they can, but they can't suture fast enough. The children have been brutalized beyond repair. The friend I made in the loony bin has all the trappings of The American Dream: A Ph.D. in sociology, a well-paying job, awards, citations, plaques, a nice apartment, handsome grown up children. Yet, because something terrible happened to her when she was a little girl, she wakes up everyday with the question Hamlet posed: To be, or not to be.

IX

I am not a victim of child abuse. However, when we moved to Richland from Kansas City in 1944, we moved right into nuclear Ground Zero. My father went to work at B-Reactor, the very first plutonium cooker that gave us Trinity and Nagasaki. We were all being fried from the get-go. Secret stuff. Butt-fucking by Uncle Sam. My siblings and I all suffer, in varying intensity, from bi-polar illness, and in the court where we were raised there were twelve cases of manic-depression in nine families. My present therapist has a theory that radiation had a dramatic effect on the thyroid gland.

X

It was on the banks of the Columbia, the Yakima and the Snake rivers that a nine-year old boy had his first visions of the marvelous: river-worn stones and radiant arrowheads. Lewis and Clark and

Sacajawea had stopped there, too, at Hanford (Chanout) and Richland (Towmowtowee). It was there that I began my Walkabout and put the sacred stone of a *word* in my mouth.

Merriwether Lewis had glimpsed the marvelous on his own Walkabout with Bill Clark. Perhaps in deep despair over helping to open the Louisiana Territory to commerce and industrialization, he put a gun to his temple back in Tennessee and ended as a suicide. ✢

Lori-ann Latrèmouille, *Jam*, charcoal on paper, 30" x 22"

SLEEPING ALONE

William Kittredge

The flashy, roving men who bought cattle had always functioned as prime liberated spirits on our edge of the West; it was their role to bring the money and make the deals. They were men on the move in big cars, living in motels, a pocketful of folding cash, wide hats, Rolex watches, and championship calf-roping buckles from their rodeo days. They would arrive in the early fall, missionaries from a state of mind in which all things, including money, were possible, and nothing, not even money, was to be taken seriously.

They, I thought, would bear some scrutiny. At once gracious and selfish, they knew the true worth of things; they had no homes, they lived nowhere we knew, they dealt in abstractions such as cows to be shipped and money to be banked. Nothing they touched was real, and they knew it. They dealt in essences.

Ours was a deeply two-hearted way of life, tied on the one hand to country and its isolations and seasons and animals, and on the other to town and money and numbers. Except for bankers and their roving bad boys, the cow buyers, few of us really understood the latter. The cow buyers knew never to put their money on justice, and thus they were to be feared, like saints; and they knew it. In their cynical, grinning, boyish death's-head way, they knew the true worth of things. It is easy to make fun of such men, but they were not fools.

I watched them, looking for clues. I was convinced that I was missing my life, and that it would be a sin, actually, to die cautious, which is to say, so dumb. I admired and envied, for instance, the wit of a friend who bought a full-scale logging truck and used it for nothing but picking up his mail. "It's like a disguise," he said. "People get so upset about your logging truck they never notice what you're really doing."

Renounce middle-class ambition, that was my notion, and I was ready, in town and edgy on long afternoons. On such occasions, techniques for self-discovery were not only life's tools, they were ways of cultivating a bad boy's dream. The beauty of afternoon light touches and dignifies each mote on the scuffed dusty floors of old barrooms.

Our shabbiest stumbling impulses from deep in the heart of the previous night turn luminous as we tell stories and laugh and get into the sauce again. This barroom life, we know, is funny and human and fragile and glorious, or at least just as all right as staying home. Or so I thought.

There is no recalling the name of the particular livestock merchant who led me through the adventures that began in the light of a particular afternoon. But I can see his face, a raffish man who would travel on a handshake, two or three clean shirts, some traveler's checks, and a reputation for getting back to you with the money. He was sitting at the bar with some friends, and they were laughing as if nothing in the world had ever been worse than a little bit foolish, and I watched them from the corner of my eye, jealous of their ease but too standoffish and frightened to attempt joining them. There was no such thing as easy familiarity, not for me, until we were maybe an hour or so into the drinking, which in the old days meant five or six quick glasses of Cutty Sark and soda, after which anything we could think of was something we ought to do.

Drinking my way into the action was a trick I had already mastered. So I was eyeing the cow buyer and his friends as potential co-conspirators. But the real center of attention that afternoon in The Indian Village was across the empty dance floor. A couple of Lake County businessmen were entertaining the women who'd come up from Reno to be their weekend guests. In short, in the words of the cow buyer, as he grinned at me and acknowledged my thanks for buying a round, "A couple of *whooors.*" He drew the word out as if he was an owl and he was hooting.

These women were thirtyish and tight-jawed, and looked to be tired of their weekend with these fat old men who were paying the freight. They were lean and would've been handsome by our standards had they got themselves up differently. But on that afternoon in Lakeview they seemed to be dressed to advertise their continuation of some unspoken deal with humiliation.

One of them was short, a little more stylishly built than the other, maybe a year or two older, but in this memory of dancing with them in the afternoon light of The Indian Village they look interchangeable. Maybe it was the eye makeup, the net stockings, and the leather-like skirts, which were constantly working up to something dark and unseeable at the crotch. Me and the cow buyer were game for an afternoon, and we were having one dance after the other, and

the men they'd come with were sitting there on the far side of the dance floor with nothing to do but watch, and it wasn't funny. Then one of them called out that it was time to go.

Me and that cow buyer were playing the jukebox and circling on the dance floor, I was smelling dangerous perfume, paired up with the younger woman, the heftier one, the quiet, softer one, some might say the dumb one, except she turned out to be smarter than me. Those potbellied businessmen were watching while we stole their dates, and we hadn't given them any way to save face. Me and the cow buyer and the so-called *whooors* were conspiring to embarrass them. I knew that much, and I would learn some more things.

I was glad to be included. The cow buyer was buying all the drinks. "Shit, kid," he said, "save your money." He was at most only five years older than me, but I was the kid. I knew it was true. He understood the way of things, and I didn't.

Anyway, to hell with those men. They had their weekend, however it was, and to hell with people in general, and their bullshit rules. Nobody cares was a program I could subscribe to without much difficulty or thought. *Fuck 'em all and sleep till noon* was a theme song people were learning to admire all over America. A revolution was taking shape, and we were part of it without even knowing it. We were just some outlandish boys in The Indian Village in Lakeview, Oregon, on the afternoon after the Labor Day Rodeo was finished, when all but a few of us were gone back to the ranch, to the job. Such was the romance.

I cannot tell you how much I admired the cow buyer when he stepped away from his dance companion and went over to stand looking down on those fellows at their table, displaying his smile like a quick show of cards. "You fellows might as well go on," he said.

"Maybe we won't," one of them said.

"Maybe I'll kick your ass." The cow buyer was still grinning, his face shining with a little whiskey sweat and his hat pushed back on his head in the fashion of a schoolyard bully. The fat men scooted around from behind the table and made their way across the empty dance floor, outside into the light, leaving us to it.

From midafternoon the action is confused for a long time, until well past dark. The four of us, me and the cow buyer and those women, we were paired up in two double beds in the only motel room available for the night at the famous Hunter's Hot Lodge on the northern edge of Lakeview. The man who rented us the room was somebody

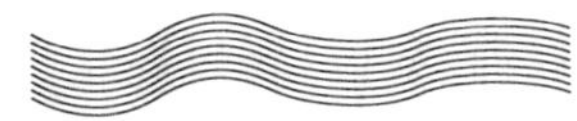

we knew. From the start he didn't like our action, but what the hell, I thought, it was a story he could tell at the barber shop.

What I recall is making love in a quick way. Not furtive, scurrying, or brutal, but quick. And isolated, more than anything: isolated, and actually alone. It was over and they were still making love in the other bed, making noises like snuffling animals on the other side of a waist-high partition. It was surprising to me that my leader, the cow buyer, would sound so childlike at anything. This was not simple fucking they were at over there. My woman on her back was gazing at the dim ceiling as if visions were playing across the cheap tiles. My isolation in that sagging bed intensified. So I put on my clothes and I went down to the large deserted barroom, where I imagined I would be a cock of the walk and deeply admired as I ordered my scotch and soda. When I looked around, nobody was paying attention, and I was back where I'd started the afternoon, alone at some bar, and deeply chilled in my being. Another run at things was over. It would lead to going home in the deep hours of night, denying guilt. It was nothing new, I saw that in my self-pity, just more of everything.

Back in our motel room, I was surprised and, at first, deeply offended. The women had changed beds. My friend the showboating cow buyer was energetically bedding the woman who'd been in my bed. They did not appear to notice the quiet opening and closing of the door. The other, the older of those women, and someone truly good in my book of memory — she was in my bed. In the flickering orange and blue light of reflected neon I could see her eyes as she lifted a hand to me. "Come on," she said, and I had enough sense to get out of my clothes and under the covers with her. I don't remember the sounds of anything other than her whispering.

"Slow down," she said, or something like that, and she started teaching me to breathe slowly, touching me everywhere in a feathery way as she did, calming my hands, persuading me that it was my duty to lie back, at least for this moment while I was learning from scratch.

What she was teaching was what we all should have learned, us boys out West, since those days. I learned that my woman in the next bed with the cow buyer had got damned little satisfaction from my thirty-five-second poke, and that was why she had moved on. She didn't owe me anything, and if I wanted allegiance I'd better learn to slow down and attend to the rewarding of someone, as someone right then was attending to me. I was learning that this dynamic is

at the heart of everything. I was learning that we should touch one another, and go out into the world smelling and tasting. I learned that I was willing, like anybody would be if they'd let themselves, once somebody told me what was what. Since then I have learned to my sadness that none of this will ever come instinctively, for reasons which likely have a lot to do with my upbringing.

But that is not the point: the point is the woman, and her anxious look as she began with me, whispering and touching, as if she was not at all certain I would be able to get beyond myself and understand anything at all, and her delight as I came easing around my distant bend into willingness, and the way her confidence grew and warmed. What I mostly recall are her attempts at perfection as she made her gifts to me. It is not, as she pointed out, something to get on with, it is the most important part of what there is.

By this time the cow buyer and the other woman were finished and they were listening and that was all right too. What we were doing felt like truth, and you had to be trusting. I didn't mind anyone listening as long as that good woman went on whispering to me and each smell and the look of her hair on the white pillow in the dim light and each movement was precisely as it should be.

And then the man who ran the motel banged on the door to run us off. "You and them whores," he shouted. This was a respectable motel, and there was going to be police and general scandal if we weren't out of there in ten minutes.

And we were. Even the cow buyer in his wide experience with power and money was terrified, so we banged around in that motel room, getting into our clothes, stomping into our boots. We buckled our buckles as the women made a pass at combing their matted hair.

There was no scandal. But for months afterwards, unable to connect, deep in the night, I would console myself with the idea that everything I wanted might be "in the wind" if I would only slow down. Not that I did. It was not possible, in such a headlong place as the working man frontiers of southeastern Oregon and northern Nevada, at least for someone so crippled in his balance as me. I was not fit to bring about any revolutions in style. Maybe I told myself something like that.

Anyway, I never said a word about such secrets to a soul. It was months before I saw the cow buyer again. We just grinned and never spoke, but we knew. I thought maybe everybody had always known, that it was only me who had to be taught. ✎

It is your wife's fortieth birthday and I am torturing you to the sounds of a tape of Dylan Thomas giving a poetry recital. His voice is theatrical and at times it scrapes at the edges of breaking into song. "Do not go gentle into that good night...," his voice rises tremulously and it is not as I hoped it would be, no rich intonations, no deep somber tones, just another poet straining to burst the threads that leash him to his existence.

"Rage, rage against the dying of the light..." Thomas screams like an invocation, and obediently I slip my foot into your mouth. You are watching me with confusion because I am drunk and wearing high heels and balancing over your naked body takes more skill than you think. I don't want to fall on you with my weight and the stabbing silver of my accouterments, injuring you, making it impossible for you to meet your wife later in the evening for dinner down by the harbor where the white ships come in and she chatters on about *The New York Review Of Books* and other things you don't understand because you decided to make money in medicine instead of writing poetry. Neither of us knew when we made our respective choices that we might be equally repressed. I do not want to hurt you, at least not clumsily, not out of drunkenness, not because the high arches of my feet prevent me from balancing in spike heels. I want it to mean something when I hurt you, I want each transgression to be a deliberate one that cuts both ways, something that neither of us will be able to blame on bottles of wine or the condition of our feet or the fact that when I am in this position, one foot balanced on your neck, there is nothing nearby to hold on to and the only thing stable is the floor which seems a long way off from up here.

I will not go gentle into you. The high heel of my shoe is in your mouth and it is cutting the roof where the flesh is ridged and ticklish. You suck the heel like something phallic and I wonder what you are tasting, what grotty remains of dust and dirt and sidewalk you are swallowing down the soft pinkness of your throat. Up here I can see you are going bald, the expanse of your forehead with your gray hair tossed backwards onto the carpet is wide and gleaming. With your eyes shut and your mouth working to please the point of my shoe, you could easily be an inflatable doll or a cartoon and I am able then to withdraw my heel as carefully as a penis and rake it in pink crescents across your cheek and down your chin.

In my sessions with you I search for the evil inside us that we exchange like tongues between our open mouths. The boundaries I once saw as steel fences in my mind turned out to be sodden smelly wooden planks when I reached them, easily kicked down. Once I even tried on myself the things I do to you. Whipping myself with a silver chain, I became fascinated by the stopped seconds of pain that opened my mouth and closed my eyes. Afterwards I was left looking down at my thighs where the circle of the chain I had snapped down my body had left a perfect imprint of itself, pink like a rubber stamp, like one of those playful rubber stamps with happy faces on them. When the pain stopped, time moved again and I saw that perhaps this was what you experienced then, this stopping of time as it raced past you now that you are middle-aged and some of your friends are already dead. "Old age should burn and rave at close of day," Thomas instructs sternly. Perhaps your life seems long only in those moments when your eyes are closed and your lips forced apart. Perhaps this is what you seek, this element of immortality, the way some people do by writing poems. I tried that day to understand what it must be like for you when the pain hits, when you protest with a convulsion in your voice that stops me because it is no longer a pleasurable pleading that runs out of your mouth like water or thin blood.

It is easy to become addicted to hurting you, to aching for that moment when you take off your clothes and lie on my floor. There is a slight roundness to your stomach and a soft field of black chest hair that sharpens into a tiger's stripe running down your belly. It looks knife-like and capable of being sadistic. I could picture you with a black beard, trying on black leather vests and turning in a mirror like the men I watch downtown in the shops I frequent now, where I finger the bewildering chains of my new trade and talk to the women behind the counter who are pierced and smiling and who recommend books that make me realize I am only on the fringe and that the depth has no bottom. You could just as easily have been one of those men who advertise for young blond slaves to torture, who read magazines that teach them how to build benches and restraints and instruments of pain. You could have turned like that and I am given to understand that perhaps one afternoon you will. Some nights I pace my apartment gently and look at the white walls and wonder whose blood is going to end up splattering this room. There is no way either of us can tell, because we are each other and there is noth-

ing restraining that moment when we exchange power like others do body fluids, saliva or semen.

The power floods into me warm and soft and golden, dusty as pollen. I had not realized previously the extent of my emptiness that no kisses could fill, no flowers or brave words of love. The emptiness sang hollow and blue and then turned red as rage. I knew from the first session that I could have killed you and that indeed you were not letting me go so far as I needed. Looking down at your muscled body on my floor, I wanted some of the red inside me to bleed out through you, in slashes and strokes of thudding color. I conceived that the pain would be clear as a sword, that the slashes across your chest and stomach would thicken and blossom like flowers, like roses.

You bought me a bracelet the other day from one of the sex shops downtown. It was sitting curled up in a dusty corner of the glass case, half-concealed by wrinkly dildos and packets of dayglo creams and lotions. I was browsing impatiently, needing to use the bathroom, my feet swelling in my heels, bored by the plastic-coated magazines and the multicolored underwear nailed to the walls. The woman behind the counter had a toothless glazed expression and eyes that looked like they were made of glass. I did not particularly want to be there and perhaps neither did you, you were lifting your watch every so often to check the time and thinking of dinner with your wife who if you were lucky might wear the red leather outfit you bought her, even if she never assumed the role. There was no time that afternoon to duck into changing rooms with burgundy lace and ripped, fringed leather skirts. The fluff no longer interested me, the delicacy of lingerie seemed an offense. It was the trickling cat o'nine tails that tickled my fingers, it was the canes perched rigid on the walls, it was even that morbid black leather mask molded to the dummy's unseeing white face on the top counter that ran currents through me. I felt as though the world I had walked on for years had flipped and on the other side there lived people who turned up palms of blood and leather.

The woman with the wrong eyes uncurled the bracelet and we saw how sharp the studs were. When she said the bracelet had been banned I said I wanted it and you paid for it and that night I fell asleep with it on my wrist while candles flickered the room in crystal holders. It tormented me all night because each time I moved my hand I would hurt myself into consciousness. The next day I wore it

and pretended it was a joke from a friend, and at lunch a man came to my table and said, You could kill somebody with that, and took it off my wrist, but then he gave it back. His eyes were brown and overly trusting. Later when I hugged my lunch companion good-bye she let out a yelp and said, You stabbed me in the back, and I smiled and looked at my wrist with its silver studs and said Yes, I am killing you with my love.

It will be a good toy for next time, applied to the more vulnerable parts of your body. I will stroke you with the eager points of the bracelet and then I will hurt you with them. That is part of the joy, the caresses that I allow before pressing down the pain. I like it best when I kiss you with full-mouthed tenderness, when I lick a finger and circle it lightly around the head of your penis, when I take one of your truncated nipples into my mouth and feel its little hard point between my teeth before I bite.

I listen to you when you call at night needing somebody to talk to and I spend half an hour with you on the phone while you talk about your marriage and your kids and your practice and I never tell you you are boring me or that my time is not for you. I show my harmlessness by giving you books of my poetry which I read to you over glasses of white wine before we hit the floor to lose our words and our regular faces.

If we are victims of each other, then in those moments we are the most beautiful victims in the world. Sometimes when I stand over you, when my heels are gouging into you, I look beyond you towards some thin line of distance and understand that each time your face wrenches with pain I am spreading a slow dark stain down the still-white years of my future, and that in that sense you are killing me and not the other way around. Each time you scream it wrings out the light in me and leaves twisted red and black cords like knotted whips lying on the wall and waiting, hungering to be used, to be applied against white skin that flinches away and cries.

You, my friend, my accomplice, my fellow victim, you have the kind of engaging smile and blue eyes that, in the daytime, makes you one of the most popular dentists in the city. You have the kind of face that patients would entrust their mouths to, the kind of fingers they would not mind probing their cavities. How could they know those same fingers take a piece of wire and wind it so tightly around the base of your penis that I wince for you? How could they know your mouth fills with everything that sifts across the bottom of high

heeled shoes that have walked the pavement? You are friendly enough, your hand cups their trusting chins, you see into them and reassure them. You see into them the way you saw into me the first night we met over drinks and lounge music, and even though I said little and at that time knew nothing, you saw something in me you described as dark, very dark, you saw a part of me I had not seen in hours of mirror reflections.

This is not a game, you kept saying until I heard it every night in my dreams. You can call it a game if you like, but I will do almost anything you want, whatever that might be.

I had thought that for me would translate into walks on the beach and poetry readings and drinking wine, that those would be the extent of my desires. I had not expected this rage that continues to grow rather than subside as you plead with me now to stop, as a thin growl rises in my throat and razors the air.

It is your wife's fortieth birthday and Dylan Thomas' voice screeches to a stop on the tape. You must leave for home and I must try to write another poem, so you edge out the door with the sun bouncing off your glasses and your briefcase tucked under your arm. I walk back into the apartment with feet that are hot and tender against the carpet, as if they might burst and your warm nourishing blood would pour out of me. I sit down at the typewriter and rub my swollen feet, their chafed heels, thinking of our obligations toward wives and poetry and thinking that perhaps this is just as well, we do not want the end to come too soon, we want to taste our pleasure bit by bit, inch by inch, we want to lick it slowly and make it last, we will make it good and make it last, my poor tiger-striped victim, we will make ourselves into people we hate enough to kill. ✍

TO SHRINK THE DISTANCES
[for Rosa]

Duane Niatum

Bitter loves drove us into seclusion.
In youth we played long and hard
the sexual dances but learned in time
to throw away the music. This spring
we offer each other the slightly hoarse
heartbeats in the ballad,
the amusing motions of candlelight
each ignites in the other's eyes.
We step back into the world's whirlwinds,
open door and window on the dormant seasons;
our skin colors like Bacchus blooms.
What we make of hunger composes itself
with the stinging nettles of longing.
We never hid the desire of our hands
and fused the shadows and the blue notes
because the myths we acted out in early
dreams were carved into our souls
with Eros' arrows. Believing the interior
stars we tango out of clothes like butterflies
mating on an apple blossom branch —
two figures plunging into darkness,
the blind alley of pleasure.

The cover art, complete: Lori-ann Latrèmouille, *Blue Woman Blue Bird*, charcoal and soft pastel, 22" x 30", 1988.

SO WHAT IF THE NEIGHBORS AREN'T HOME

Peter Sears

The flight ends when the plane touches down.
No, she replies, when the plane comes to a halt.
Actually, he adds, when you come through the
passageway into the airport; that's your first
solid ground. Why not, she asks, when you get
your baggage? Because you may not have any
baggage, and he about breaks into song. Look
she declares, before you bust out of your pants,
let me say the flight ends when you get home.

You fuddy duddy, he yelps, just when we were
getting going! She tilts her head and singsongs,
Sore head, sore loser. We are rolling! he roars,
let's get the neighbors over and have a time!
Just what she wanted to hear, the neighbors
aren't home. So what if he leaves a dumb message
on their phone machine, she'll put on a record
and juggle her shoes. Dumb old rock and roll,
crank it up, sway, and kiss until it hurts.

When you first floated an hello to my hello,

you lifted the lid of my skin

and came in. Now, when you leave,

I'm inside out. I drive to find a place

to drive. The road hisses to the rain,

curls its toes. It knows, the park

will pull me over unless, right now,

I kiss you again here and there and there

and lose my hands in your rolling hair.

DOWN A WELL

Peter
Sears

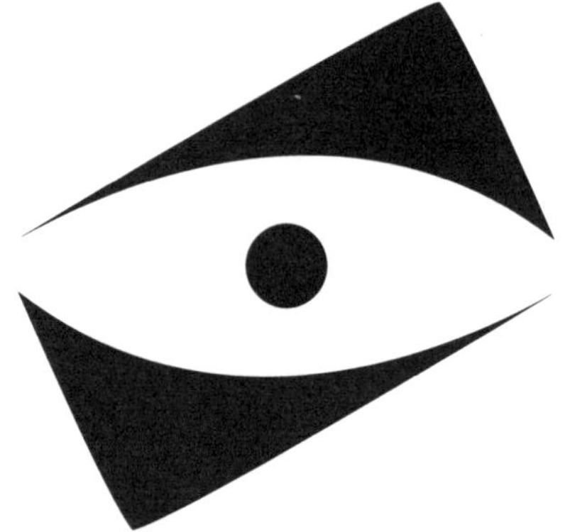

Jim Aho is a first generation American whose father emigrated from Finland around 1920 and settled in Aberdeen along the Wishkah River. Local legend likens the river to a salmon. Why? "Because there's 'Fins' on both sides." The Finnish people generally are alleged to have descended from the ancient Israelite tribe of Issachar, according to Identity Christian mythology. "Aho" refers to a small forest meadow of the kind frequently seen in the Cascades, deep pine grass surrounded by tall black evergreens, perhaps sundered by a sand-bottomed clear brook. "The story of Ed and Lisa Minor is taken from my book *The Politics of Righteousness* (University of Washington Press, 1991); that of Greg Withrow from my forthcoming sequel to this book, entitled *The Enemy: Its Social Construction and Deconstruction*." Jim is a professor of Sociology at Idaho State University in Pocatello.

Kathleen Alcalá's first collection of short stories, *Mrs. Vargas and the Dead Naturalist,* was recently published by Calyx Books. She is currently researching her tribe and family for a historical novel. The first sex scene she ever wrote was published in *ERGO!* in conjunction with her reading at Bumbershoot 1992.

Judith Barrington is the author of two collections of poetry: *Trying to be an Honest Woman* (1985) and *History and Geography* (1989), which was a finalist for the Oregon Book Awards, and editor of *An Intimate Wilderness: Lesbian Writers on Sexuality* (1991). She is currently working on a book of memoirs about Spain, for which she received a creative nonfiction grant from the Oregon Institute of Literary Arts. She lives in Portland with her partner of 13 years, Ruth Gundle.

Seattle photographer **Marsha Burns** often photographs people she encounters on the streets. She worked with a Polaroid 20x24 camera in New York and Frankfurt. Marsha uses primarily natural light and is currently working from negatives for a series titled "Portraits from America." A book of her work, *Postures,* was published by the Friends of Photography in 1982, and her photographs are in the permanent collections of more than 35 museums in the U.S. and abroad.

Omar Castañeda: "I am male, one of five children, and Guatemalan — naturalized USA citizen at age eleven. My family is the first generation in this country, so that half the children were born in Guatemala, half in the USA. My writing is often a search for my heri-

tage, for some way to understand the clash of cultures, the mixed political allegiances within me. I have two novels, *Cunuman* and *Among the Volcanoes*, a sequel due out late 1993, and a picture book, *Abuela's Weave*, due spring 1993." Omar teaches creative writing at Western Washington University in Bellingham.

René Denfeld is a Portland-based writer. She has written for several publications, including *The New Times*, *Pitch*, *Creative Loafing*, *The Riverfront Times*, and *PDXS*. She is currently working on a book about young women and feminism for Warner Books. Family? She has one. Tribe? She doesn't know what that means. Sex? None of your business.

Margaret Dragu is a writer, performer, film maker, video artist, choreographer, and mother. She lives with her partner and her daughter, Aretha, on the south arm of the Fraser River in British Columbia.

David Duncan: "I am the author of two novels, *The Brothers K* (Doubleday '92 & Bantam, next summer) and *The River Why* (Sierra Club '83 & Bantam' 84). My stories and essays have appeared in *Zyzzyva*, *Rotund World*, *Harper's*, *The North American Review*, and *Gray's Sporting Journal*. I am a lifelong anti-industrialist who nevertheless owns a computer and a car, a proponent of economic secession who nevertheless pays taxes, a distruster of international conglomerates with a publisher owned by a West German conglomerate, a devout closet mystic (love God, loathe proselytizing), and pretty dang decent fly fisherman. I live in Oregon and elsewhere with the ceramic sculptor, Adrian Arleo, and our 2.5 children."

Martha Gies: "Mine was originally the tribe of wanderers and dreamers; in 1983 I joined the tribe of social activist Catholics. The first Gies youth to arrive in Oregon came from Austria in the mid-19th century and went to the Bohemia Mountains looking for gold. My sexual persona is curing itself of an early fascination with Marlene Dietrich."

Cartoonist **Matt Groening** grew up in Portland, Oregon and attended Evergreen State College in Washington. In an interview with *The Comics Journal*, he says: "I just remember as a kid being fascinated by the extremes of human endeavor, and mostly the negative extremes — death and violence and morbid kinds of things — because that's what unnerves people the most." In speaking about his work, Matt continues: "When I got the opportunity to draw my comic, I wanted to do what was on my mind, the stuff that keeps me worried: love, work, sex, death — the basics. I was always

amazed that so many cartoons either dealt with political ideas in a very heavy-handed way, or concentrated on the trivial inconsequentialities of life, while the hellishness of most people's jobs and love lives and fear of death remain unexplored."

Andy Helman has been a commercial and public television broadcasting writer, producer, and talent for more years than she will cop to. A journalism major who never truly defected from the printed word, her work has appeared in such diverse publications as *Cosmopolitan* and the *Christian Science Monitor*. A baby boomer who hasn't adjusted to the '90s, Andy has often pondered the possibility her lineage may be traced to one of Israel's 10 lost tribes.

Anndee Hochman's essay is part of a book-in-progress, *Essential Outlaws: Women Exploring Kinship,* to be published in the fall of 1993 by The Eighth Mountain Press of Portland, Oregon. Anndee is a freelance writer whose articles, essays, reviews, and short fiction have appeared recently in *Ms. Magazine, The Oregonian, Glimmer Train Stories,* and *Short Fiction by Women*. She is a former Washington Post metro reporter. Anndee is pleased that her family bears not even a remote resemblance to the GOP ideal.

Lawson Fusao Inada is the author of two books of poetry: *Before the War*, Morrow, 1971, and *Legends From Camp*, Coffee House Press, 1992. He is an editor of two Asian-American anthologies: *AIIIEEEEE!* and *THE BIG AIIIEEEEE!*, and is an English professor at Southern Oregon State College. Regarding sex, family, tribe — "Among all the distinctions we have, and make, I like to remember what my Tibetan Buddhist teacher said: 'We have all been parents of each other.'"

Ken Kesey, who lives in Oregon, wrote *One Flew Over the Cuckoo's Nest, Sometimes a Great Notion, Kesey's Garage Sale, Demon Box*, and *The Further Inquiry*. In an Esquire interview with Chip Brown, he says of *Sailor Song*: "I think people turned right and headed to Alaska — to go beyond the periphery of culture and society...I see it almost like a comic book — really broad lines sometimes show more truth than really finely nuanced lines. I think of readers more and more as viewers...I'm writing for the MTV audience — you have to have quick cuts, brightly colored shots, to hold them."

William Kittredge is the author of two collections of stories – *The Van Gogh Field* and *We Are Not in This Together* – and a book of essays, *Owning It All*. With Annick Smith, he edited *The Last Best Place: A Montana Anthology*. He lives in Missoula, Montana.

147

Lori-ann Latrèmouille lives in Vancouver, B.C., and is represented by the Augen Gallery in Portland, Oregon. She has also had shows in Western Canada, Seattle, and Switzerland. Her art will be shown next year in cultural centers in Hong Kong and Tokyo.

Evelyn Lau: "I was born in Vancouver (B.C.) in 1971. I am the author of three books: *Runaway: Diary of a Street Kid* (Harper Collins, autobiography), *You Are Not Who You Claim* (Press Porcepic, poetry) and *Oedipal Dreams* (Beach Holme, poetry). *Runaway* was a Canadian bestseller and will be filmed as a CBC Television movie. I left home at fourteen, and having worked as a prostitute I tend to explore the darker, more perverse regions of sexuality in my work. I am not interested in writing pornography or even erotica; I am more interested in the psychology behind sexual behavior, and the issues of power and abuse."

Ursula K. Le Guin biostats:

> Sex: Yes.
> Family: Very strange, just like yours.
> Tribe: Sinshan Kesh.
> Recent books: *Searoad* (fiction) and a revised edition of *Language of the Night* (essays) (Both Harper Collins)

Doug Marx is a poet, freelance journalist, teacher, professional land surveyor, and family man. His poems have appeared in such publications as *COLUMBIA — a Magazine of Poetry & Prose, Hubbub, Mississippi Mud*, and *Alaska Quarterly Review*. He's a frequent contributor to the *Oregonian, Willamette Week*, and *Writer's NW*, and his essays on A.B. Guthrie and William Stafford appeared in *Left Bank #1*.

Colleen J. McElroy: "I found that as a black woman, writing, like traveling, demands patience and surprise, rebellion and conformity, the kindness of strangers sprinkled with a little imagination and a lot of observation. I write out of the impressions of a St. Louis born African-American, a former Army dependent, a speech pathologist turned poet and fiction writer, a folklorist, a woman who cannot, who will not, stay put. The truth is, I have spent my life traveling from somewhere to the next place. When my mother asks me : Why do you go to all those places?, my answer still is: Because they are there." McElroy's latest publications are *Driving Under the Cardboard Pines*(fiction), and *What Madness Brought Me Here: New and Selected Poems, 1968-88*. This memoir is one of a collection begun at Rockefeller Center in Bellagio Italy.

Diane Meili is the great granddaughter of Victoria Callihoo, a well-known Cree elder. Before writing her book, *Those Who Know: Profiles of Alberta's Native Elders*, she was editor of *Windspeaker*, Alberta's bi-weekly Native newspaper, published in Edmonton. She currently lives in Peace River.

Duane Niatum (Klallam tribe of Washington State) recently published his fifth volume of poetry, *Drawings of the Song Animals: New And Selected Poems*, (Duluth, MN: Holy Cow Press, 1991). *Songs for the Harvester of Dreams*, published in 1981 by the University of Washington Press won The Before Columbus Foundation American Book Award in 1982. He edited *Carriers of the Dream Wheel* (1975) an anthology for Harper & Row, which is considered the most widely read and known book on contemporary American Indian poetry.

Raised by televisions in the 1960s, **Lucia Maria Perillo** is now trying to wean herself from electronic culture cold turkey. Her formative influences were female spin offs like The Girl From U.N.C.L.E. and Batgirl, who can even now be seen on syndicated TV in Mexico, where she is dubbed with the name Bat Chica.

Recent poems by **Peter Sears** have appeared in the *Atlantic, Cimarron Review,* and *Poet & Critic.* Forthcoming poems are in *Antioch Review, Calapooya Collage, Northwest Review, Orion Nature Quarterly,* and a Milkweed Press anthology of driving poems. His most recent book is *Gonna Bake Me A Rainbow Poem*, a national anthology of high-school student poetry from Scholastic Inc. He works for the Oregon Arts Commission and lives with his wife Anita Helle in the country outside of Corvallis.

William Stafford: "Just this morning I was thinking that people ally themselves and have allegiances because of insignificant things like remote ancestors, or skin color, or place, or political links, and so on. More important are immediate, daily preferences and characteristics we freight around all our lives, ineluctably linked with others of our kind. So — these might identify me: — short, quiet, dark, left-handed, ironic, evasive. Some people tend to look and listen. I like to smell things. In a roomful of people, I tend to join those near a window or a door, no matter what their other characteristics are. We take a look or sniff and recognize each other as belonging to a tribe that you have to be part of to recognize." Recent publications: *The Animal That Drank Up Sound,* (a children's book, illustrated by Debra Frasier), Harcourt, Brace, Jovanovich, 1992. *My Name Is William Tell,* Confluence Press, 1992. *Seeking the Way,* (with illuminations by Robert Johnson), Melia Press, Minneapolis, 1992.

After dropping out of Princeton, **Clemens Starck** continued his education on the road traveling and working. He was a ranch hand in eastern Oregon, a newspaper reporter on Wall Street, a merchant seaman, and a student of Chinese, among other things. A collection of his work, *Journeyman's Wages*, is scheduled for publication in 1993 by Story Line Press. Starck lives with his wife and three teenage children in the foothills of the Coast Range, south of Dallas, Oregon.

Born in California and raised in Hawaii, **Kathleen Tyau** lives on a farm in North Plains, Oregon. "My Chinese mother insisted a horse doctor delivered me. She blamed him for the 'cauliflower' fold in my right ear, where his forceps fell. I pictured a stable with straw, flies, and horses until I saw the name of the California hospital on my birth certificate. Now I realize she was trying to describe the rudeness she felt as the white country doctor in a cow town reached into her private parts with his thick, hairy hands. Her family lived over three thousand miles away in Hawaii, far from my first home, a trailer on the college campus where my father studied. When I visit her graveyard in Hawaii, I take flowers instead of food and whiskey, but I am careful not to mention living on a farm."

Bill Witherup is the author of *Black Ash, Orange Fire, The Collected Poems 1959-1985*, Floating Island Publications, 1986, and *Men at Work*, Ahsahta Press, 1990. He is also represented in the Hanford Downwinder Traveling Exhibit, sponsored by Washington Physicians for Social Responsibility, and he is an active volunteer for WPSR.

WINTER 1993   Issue 5

GLIMMER TRAIN

Stories by Sigrid Nunez, James English, Elizabeth Judd,
Lee Martin, Lawson Fusao Inada, Mary Ellis, Robert Abel,
Susan Alenick, Gary Wilson, Susan Burmeister.

Interviews with writers
William Styron and Joyce Thompson.

3 4 >

U.S. $9.00
Canada $13.00
£7.00
I£6.20

Writer Detained:
Gustavo Guzman
by Siobhan Dowd

E V E R Y M A N ' S
L I B R A R Y

THE PERFECT GIFT FOR YOURSELF,
A FRIEND, AND YOUR CHILDREN.

Start a library with the world's greatest writers available in affordable, beautifully produced, hardcover editions. Over 100 new titles in all. Visit your local bookstore.

Austen ♦ Bronte ♦ Cather ♦ Dickens
Homer ♦ Joyce ♦ Milton ♦ Mann
Shakespeare ♦ Tolstoy ♦ Trollope
Twain ♦ Woolf

and many others

Each book in the Everyman's Library is printed on acid-free, wove paper with full-cloth sewn bindings and silk ribbon-marker.

Published by Knopf

FAMILY PORTRAITS IN CHANGING TIMES

Family Portraits in Changing Times profiles a cross section of families through photographs and personal stories, offering insights and greater understanding into the constellation of new families in the U.S. The families in this book represent a variety of interpersonal, interdependent relationships, including multiracial, multigenerational, divorced, single, step-family, physically disabled, adopted, gay, or lesbian.

By Helen Nestor
Foreword by
Judith Stacey, Ph.D.

30 Family Portraits
144 pages, 9" x 12"

Softcover $22.95
ISBN 0-939165-15-5

Clothbound $39.95
ISBN 0-939165-16-3

Helen Nestor has been photographing families since the 1970s. Her work has been published in books and magazines, and her photographs exhibited internationally. Judith Stacey is an author and family scholar, as well as a professor of sociology and women's studies at UC Davis.

To order, send check
or money order to:

FREE SHIPPING

NEWSAGE PRESS

P.O. Box 607
Troutdale, OR 97060-0607
(503) 232-6794   Fax: (503) 232-6891

LEFT BANK

A new way to read between the lines — a potlatch of pointed prose and poetry.

Publishers Weekly called it "uniformly excellent." The *LA Times Book Review* said, "...sharply focused essays...visual elegance." *Library Journal* stated: "...an exceptionally well-edited entry into information and a joy for all of us." Semiannual in December & June, **LEFT BANK** is a book series featuring NW writers on universal themes. Readers are treated to a provocative, entertaining, and evocative cross-section of creative nonfiction, fiction, essays, interviews, poetry, and art.

Themes are determined by an editorial staff and advisory board of respected writers, editors, and publishers from Alaska, British Columbia, Idaho, Montana, Oregon, and Washington.

#1: Writing & Fishing the Northwest — features the likes of Wallace Stegner, Craig Lesley, Sharon Doubiago, Greg Bear, Nancy Lord, and John Keeble.

#2: Extinction — read it before it disappears. David Suzuki introduces Barry Lopez, David Quammen, Tess Gallagher, Sallie Tisdale, Robert Michael Pyle, John Callahan, Nancy Lord, and others.

#3: Sex, Family, Tribe — it's in your hand. Enjoy.

#4: Gotta Earn a Living — opening with an interview with Gary Snyder, the theme of work is explored from many perspectives by a cast of fine writers.

LEFT BANK

— a great gift to give yourself or any thoughtful friend who enjoys the adventure of superb writing. Just photocopy this page, fill in the form below, and send it today.

Subscriptions are $14, postage paid, and begin with the next issue/edition to be published, but back issues are available for $7.95 plus $2 shipping and handling.

Send **LEFT BANK** to me at:

Send a gift subscription to:

I'd like the following back issues:

My order total is:

I've enclosed a check or Money Order — or charge my VISA or MC; its number and expiration are: